SELF-NURTURANCE:

Route to Emotional Wellbeing and Resilience

Minu Singh Joshi

Cover Design by Mukul Gijare

Saanvi and Shirish, Your unwavering belief in me and endless patience have kept me on track. I cannot imagine this journey without you; you've been instrumental in making this book a reality!

Mukul and Rajeev, I am truly grateful to you. Your motivating words and humor always brighten up my day.

A special mention to Mukul for putting up with my numerous corrections and tantrums while working on the cover page.

And Amigo, My furry writing buddy. Thanks for always being around me; you are indeed a paw-some partner.

FOREWORD

I feel proud and grateful as I write the foreword for this book. I have known Minu for the past 24 years and have witnessed her transformation from a buddy to a successful psychologist and life coach who positively impacts the lives of many.

In this book, she discusses self-nurturing in an accessible way, allowing readers to connect easily. Here, she teaches us to pay attention to ourselves without feeling guilty.

It conveys a deeper, simpler message: **"I matter too."**

Minu emphasizes that self-nurturance does not need external validation. Instead, delve within and discover yourself. It is not a destination but an ongoing journey.

One can take charge of one's journey, prioritize wellbeing and personal growth, and build a strong foundation to align actions with goals.

I want to recommend this book to everyone, not just

because Minu wrote it, but because it helps us transform our lives and practice self-nurturance in a very easy and simple manner.

Shirish Sj

I've known Minu my whole life, mostly because she is my mother. I have seen the hard work and dedication she has put into this book, using her years of experience as a psychologist and a mother. She combines ancient Indian wisdom and modern scientific research to give us a clear path toward self-nurturance

As someone who reads more fiction than non-fiction, I found it very easy to digest this book, because of the clear and concise manner in which she has written it. She uses various examples and relatable scenarios to help us understand the value of self-nurturance.

For many people, self-nurturance seems like a huge task, a selfish thing. In this book, Minu destroys these myths and talks about not just the importance of self-nurturance but how to implement it in your daily life. Self-nurturance is not a project that you have to undertake, just some small and easy steps towards living the life you want.

Self-nurturance is not putting yourself above others but rather allowing yourself to receive the same kind of love and care you give to the people you care about. In fact, by nurturing yourself, you will have an abundance of positive energy to share with everyone around you, making your relationships stronger and your life more fulfilled.

Saanvi Msj

Acknowledgement

As I write this acknowledgement, I feel immense gratitude for everyone who has influenced the journey of Self-Nurturance: Route to Emotional Wellbeing and Resilience. This book represents more than just a collection of ideas; it's a mosaic of experiences, lessons, and inspirations drawn from life and the remarkable individuals I've had the honor of encountering throughout this journey.

To all of you, who have inspired and supported me throughout this journey, your presence has been like sunlight filtering through dense trees, providing clarity, direction, and warmth when I needed it most.

To my clients, each of you has been a guiding light on this journey. Your courage in facing life's challenges, your willingness to explore the depths of your inner self, and your trust in me have profoundly inspired me. You have shown that healing is not just a goal but a courageous act—an embrace of your inner brilliance. Through your stories of resilience, I have gained just as much insight as I've shared, and this book reflects those invaluable lessons. Thank you for continually reminding me that self-nurturance speaks the universal language of love, starting from within and extending outward.

To my readers, this book was crafted for you; the seekers, healers, and wanderers longing for a deeper connection to yourselves. You are the essence of this work, and I hope these pages offer a safe space and a gentle guide on your journey. Thank you for allowing me to walk alongside you, even briefly, in your quest for emotional wellbeing and resilience.

To my family and friends, the roots that ground me and the branches that support me during my storms of self-doubt: your unwavering belief in my vision has been the light on my darkest nights.

To my mentors and guides—those who have crossed my path and those who emerged as life lessons during challenging times—your support has been a compass, keeping me true to my purpose.

A special thank you to the invisible yet undeniable energy of life that shaped this book — the meditations in stillness, the long walks, the lessons learned in moments of despair, the wisdom whispered through failures, and the unspoken truths discovered in silence. I learned that resilience is not a destination but a dance; it is the rhythm of falling and rising, breaking and becoming, surrendering and soaring.

And finally, to myself—the part of me that dreamed of creating something meaningful, who stumbled and got back up, who doubted but kept writing—thank you. You are living proof that self-nurturance is not a luxury; it is a necessity, a gift we give ourselves that radiates into every aspect of life.

This book is my offering to the world, a seed sown in the hope of blossoming into a garden within the hearts of those who need it. May it serve as a reminder that you hold an endless source of love, resilience, and light within. You're your own healer, your personal sanctuary, and your own wellspring of strength.

With deepest gratitude and love,

Minu

उद्धरेदात्मनात्मानं नात्मानमवसादयेत् ।

आत्मैव ह्यात्मनो बन्धुरात्मैव रिपुरात्मनः ॥

Uddhared Atmanātmānaṁ nātmānam avasādayet,
Atmaiva hyātmano bandhur ātmaiva ripur ātmanaḥ.

(*Bhagavad Gita* 6.5)

"Lift yourself by yourself; do not let yourself down. For you alone are your friend, and you alone are your enemy."

This verse eloquently expresses the core of self-nurturance. It highlights the significance and duty we hold in looking after ourselves and the transformative power that arises from connecting with our inner selves.

CONTENTS

Introduction: A Way Forward

The Journey Begins

CHAPTER **1**

Let us Dive Deeper...

CHAPTER 2

Lack of Self-Nurturance: Impact on Self and Others

CHAPTER 3

Self-Nurturance: The Surrounding Myths and Facts

CHAPTER 4

Pathways to Self-Nurturance for Wellbeing and Resilience

CHAPTER 5

The Transformative Power of Self- Nurturance

CHAPTER 6

Do- It- Yourself Self- Nurturance Practices

CHAPTER 7

Make Self-Nurturance Sustainable

CHAPTER 8

Spread the Goodness: Inspire Others to Embrace Self-Nurturance

CHAPTER 9

Gratitude

INTRODUCTION

A WAY FORWARD...

*"To understand yourself is the beginning of wisdom." –
J. Krishnamurti*

Every journey begins with a moment—an awakening, a choice, a whisper from within that says: There must be another way!

Perhaps that moment has led you to this book and these words. You may have felt the world's weight pressing down, a silent ache that is familiar yet hard to define. You might be weathering life's storms, holding onto the hope of calmer seas ahead. Or perhaps you are simply seeking ways to live with more peace, resilience, and a profound connection to yourself.

No matter why you chose this book, I want you to know

that you are precisely where you need to be.

Throughout my years as a mental health professional and life coach, I have had the privilege of supporting numerous individuals as they navigated their challenges, uncovered their strengths, and discovered new ways to nurture themselves that they had never imagined. From these experiences, as well as my own, I have learned that self-nurturance is not merely a skill; it is essential to our wellbeing. It serves as the bedrock for emotional health and resilience. Despite this, many of us find it difficult to prioritize self-nurturance.

We live in a society that values productivity more than peace, prioritizes sacrifice over self-nurturance, and regards resilience as a virtue exclusively attained through hardship. We hear advice to "push through," "stay strong," and "keep going" despite our inner selves yearning for rest, contemplation, and rejuvenation.

Here is the reality: resilience does not mean enduring pain until you break. It involves learning to flex, adapt, and nurture yourself, ensuring you never reach that breaking point.

Resilience is about cultivating a compassionate, curious, and caring relationship with yourself, one that empowers you not only to survive but also to thrive truly.

This book invites you to foster that relationship.

In the upcoming chapters, we will delve into the essence of self-nurturance: route to your emotional wellbeing and resilience with the same love and attention you readily give to others. Together, we will discover practical tools, reflective exercises, and empowering insights that enable you to cultivate a life that is grounded, fulfilling, and authentically your own.

This journey goes beyond just mastering the techniques or ticking off tasks. It focuses on transformation: changing how you perceive yourself, your needs, and your values. It is about fostering inner strength that arises not from battling yourself but from connecting with your true self.

Consider this book a map, not a fixed roadmap, but a versatile guide designed to help you navigate your unique landscape. Inside, you will discover reflective prompts, inspiring stories, and supportive strategies, yet the route you take will be entirely your own. Ultimately, self-nurturance is not a standard journey; it's profoundly personal because each individual is distinctly unique.

Remember this as you go through these pages: You don't need to have everything figured out. There is not a "right way" to self-nurturance or a "perfect" form of resilience. All that is needed is the readiness to start, to take one small step towards the life you deserve, and then another, and another.

If you're feeling confused or overwhelmed, remember that you're not alone. This book is not meant to dictate who you should be or what actions to take. Instead, it is here to accompany you, provide guidance, and help you recall the truths that many of us have lost sight of:

You deserve love, particularly from yourself!

As you embark on this journey, I encourage you to approach it with an open heart and a curious mind. Allow yourself to rest as needed, explore what speaks to you, and release what doesn't. Have faith that every step, no matter how small, is a step forward!

The path ahead isn't about achieving perfection; it's about making progress. It's about embracing yourself in each moment and uncovering the deep strength that arises from nurturing your true self.

I greet you with warmth and support as you embark on this journey.

I still recall the day I first met her, Areha (name changed). She entered my consulting room with a smile that failed to reach her eyes. Her shoulders sagged under the unseen burden of something she couldn't yet articulate. As she settled on the couch opposite me, she nervously scanned the room as if searching for answers to questions still unformed.

"I just feel… lost," she finally confessed, her voice scarcely above a whisper.

In that moment, Areha reminded me of many people I've encountered, not only clients but also friends, colleagues, and even myself at times. It's a feeling we all face at some point: that unsettling feeling of disconnection, much like a traveler stranded at a crossroads without a map, uncertain which path might lead them home.

I listened as Areha recounted her story. The weight of work pressures, demanding relationships, and unfulfilled expectations loomed over her. She described how she poured everything into others, leaving her feeling empty. Somewhere along the journey, she had forgotten to nurture her heart and nourish her spirit.

"Where do I even begin?" she asked, her voice trembling.

That's when I mentioned something that seemed to shift the atmosphere in the room:

"You start here. With yourself."

This simple truth that all journeys of healing, growth, and resilience begin with self-nurturance lies at the heart of my work as a mental health professional and life coach. It's a reality I've come across repeatedly in stories like Areha's and my own life. Yet, it's often neglected in a world that prizes busyness and self-sacrifice, where taking time for oneself is frequently labelled as selfish or indulgent.

As Areha and I continued our conversation, I introduced a metaphor I often employ: life resembles a garden. Without proper care, watering, weeding, and nourishing the roots, it starts to fade. We might try to distract ourselves by tending to the needs of other gardens, giving away our time and energy, but inevitably, we end up standing in our own patch of barren earth, questioning why nothing thrives.

The road to emotional wellbeing and resilience isn't about repairing something broken; it's about returning to oneself, nurturing neglected parts, and building a robust foundation capable of withstanding life's storms. This journey isn't straightforward, nor is it always easy. But it is worth it!

In the following weeks, I witnessed Areha beginning to reconnect with her true self. She started small, dedicating a few minutes each day to doing something that brought her joy, writing her thoughts down or simply enjoying silent moments while listening to music.

Over time, those small acts of self-nurturance evolved into a practice that began transforming her life.

I won't claim that Areha's story concluded perfectly, with a fairy-tale ending. Life isn't a storybook. Challenges and moments of doubt persisted. But a shift had occurred.

Areha discovered her inner compass, the part capable of guiding her back to herself, regardless of how far she had wandered.

Thus, her journey, along with those of many others like her, became the inspiration for this book.

As you flip through these pages, remember that this is not merely Areha's narrative. It's yours as well. It represents anyone who has ever felt lost, overwhelmed, or disconnected. It's about rediscovering yourself, nurturing your wounded parts, and cultivating resilience that will propel you forward.

The journey starts here, not with a map, but with a single step.

So, before you embark on this journey, I invite you to pause for a moment. Breathe deeply. Close your eyes if it feels right. Ask yourself: What do I need right now?

Perhaps it's rest, reassurance, or simply the permission to release the idea that everything must already be figured out.

Whatever it may be, understand that this is the beginning of your journey, not with perfection, but with intention; not with answers, but with curiosity; not with grand gestures, but with gentle acts of self-love.

Welcome to this path of self-nurturance. May it lead you to a stronger, more resilient self and a profound understanding of who you are and all you can become.

Because, like Areha, you already possess everything you need within you.

Let's set forth on the journey of "Self-Nurturance: Route to Emotional Wellbeing and Resilience."

CHAPTER 1

LET US DIVE DEEPER...

Wanting to reform the world without discovering one's true Self is like trying to cover the world with leather to avoid the pain of walking on stones and thorns. It is much simpler to wear shoes.

— *Ramana Maharshi*

We have made significant progress from a time when mere survival was humanity's only worry. Now, the focus has shifted from just staying alive to genuinely living, pursuing happiness, fulfilment, and emotional stability.

However, as I contemplate the concept of self-nurturance, an intriguing paradox arises.

As humans, we are biologically programmed to

safeguard our wellbeing. This survival instinct, refined over centuries of evolution, compels us to pursue safety, nourishment, and shelter. It functions as a natural mechanism that has allowed us to withstand challenges and adjust to a constantly evolving environment. Our species' resilience greatly depends on this inherent motivation.

Yet, here lies the paradox:

If we are naturally inclined to nurture ourselves at the fundamental level, then why does self-nurturance—the deliberate act of attending to our emotional and mental wellbeing—seem so difficult to grasp?

Why do we frequently overlook our own needs, opting to prioritize others instead? It feels like standing before a source of refreshment yet choosing to turn away, thirsty.

The answer may be rooted in the evolution of modern life.

Unlike our ancestors, who confronted immediate physical threats, we now grapple with more nuanced challenges that can be just as exhausting. We contend with unseen enemies such as chronic stress, societal expectations, and the unending drive for success. In our pursuit of achievement and provision, we often overlook the need to take a moment to recharge.

Imagine a tree rising amidst a vibrant city, its roots striving to locate fertile soil among the concrete and cacophony. It stands strong because it has to, yet its leaves start to fade as time passes, and its branches grow frail. Without adequate nourishment, even the hardiest tree struggles to flourish. In the same way, our emotional wellbeing demands intentional maintenance, necessitating a profound nurturing of our inner selves.

Self-nurturance encourages a new understanding of resilience. It isn't merely about tolerating pain or enduring fatigue. Real resilience involves knowing the right moments to pause, rest, and rejuvenate. This means realizing that thriving involves more than mere survival; it necessitates honoring the delicate balance between effort and wellbeing renewal.

This encourages us to examine not only how to live but

also how to truly thrive. It is a journey of rediscovery where we reconnect with the simple but significant truth: We deserve the same sensitivity and compassion that we generously offer to others.

It invites us to delve further, exploring not only to survive but to *flourish*.

Unveiling Your Authentic Self: An Inner Exploration

Have you ever taken a moment to reflect and ask yourself:

Who am I, truly?

What do I want beyond societal expectations?

What does my heart genuinely seek?

What unifies my life's purpose?

These questions are like soft whispers urging us to look inward and contemplate.

But how frequently do we actually pause, put everything

aside, and listen?

For many of us, life seems like a never-ending act. We assume the roles of caregivers, problem-solvers, achievers, and many more, expanding our energy to meet the needs of our children, partners, parents, friends, colleagues, and so on and so forth.

Although we thrive in responding to external pressures, we frequently disconnect from our inner selves.

We understand the aspirations and requirements of those we care for while our own desires linger unexamined, seeking acknowledgement.

Life's external focus undoubtedly brings its benefits. However, there are times when we need to turn our attention inward, transitioning from taking action in the world to being present with ourselves. This internal journey doesn't demand significant effort; it starts with small, intentional actions: taking brief pauses amidst the day's hustle to sit in silence, reflect, and breathe.

In these instances, we reconnect with our inner selves, the part of us that possesses the wisdom and clarity we often seek outside ourselves.

The journey of self-discovery starts now. It begins with genuinely listening to your inner self. The decisions you've made, the beliefs you embrace, and the dreams you cherish or neglect have all contributed to the life you experience today.

If you seek change and desire to align with your innermost desires, it must start from within. Transformation is about nurturing the core of your being, not merely altering external situations.

Self-nurturance involves fostering an inner environment that promotes growth, healing, and fulfilment. By nurturing your thoughts, beliefs, and self-perception, you establish a foundation for significant change in your external life. This embodies intentional living: understanding that your internal self-nurturance influences the external life you create.

Here is your invitation, a gentle call to pause and turn inward!

Take a moment today to sit in silence with yourself.

Consider the questions you've been too busy to think about.

What do you truly need?

What gives you joy?

What dreams have you set aside, and how might you start to nurture them again?

As you reflect, you'll discover that the answers have always been within you, simply waiting for you to acknowledge them.

This journey focuses on reconnecting with and honoring your true self. It emphasizes nurturing yourself with the same commitment you have extended to others.

Start small. Take a step today to reestablish your connection with yourself. This marks the beginning of your awakening, a path of self-discovery and nurturance.

Let us explore together what it means to come home to yourself and create a life that truly reflects who you are.

Understanding Self-Nurturance

Have you ever noticed how effortlessly nature nurtures itself?

The sun rises each morning without hesitation, rivers flow along their paths without needing approval, and trees willingly shed their leaves to make way for fresh growth. Similarly, self-nurturance involves reclaiming your right to prioritize yourself intentionally, unapologetically, and with kindness.

I have come to view self-nurturance as a fundamental element of emotional wellbeing and resilience. It is not about occasional pampering or fleeting indulgences; instead, it involves cultivating a lasting, nurturing relationship with yourself that is grounded in love and intention.

Self-nurturance is a commitment to nourish every aspect of yourself: your body, mind, heart, and spirit. It involves recognizing that we are not machines created to operate endlessly on productivity but living beings who need time to rest, heal, and grow.

That said, let's be honest: The idea of self-nurturance may seem unfamiliar or even unsettling. We live in a culture that often glorifies self-sacrifice and constant hustle. We have been conditioned to equate our worth with the extent of our contributions to others, often sacrificing our own needs in the process. In this environment, prioritizing your own wellbeing can appear selfish, indulgent, or even inappropriate.

Yet, I assure you: it is not!

Self-nurturance is not about putting yourself above others. It is about including yourself in the circle of nurture and compassion that you willingly extend to everyone else. It involves recognising that your needs are just as valid and important as those of the people you love and giving yourself permission to meet those needs without guilt or shame.

It begins with a simple question: **What do I need to feel complete?**

To truly listen to your inner self—the part of you often overshadowed by the daily demands of life—is the first step. When you ask that question and respond with kindness instead of judgment, you create an opportunity for a deeper, more compassionate relationship with yourself.

Self-nurturance encourages you to prioritize your wellbeing, not as an act of indulgence but as a necessity for a balanced and fulfilling life.

Understanding the Core of Self-Nurturance: What Does It Mean?

At its core, self-nurturance revolves around the concept of connection. It involves the continual practice of engaging with yourself, your emotions, feelings, thoughts, body, and soul.

The question might seem simple, yet answering it often requires thoughtful reflection. Many of us have spent years neglecting our needs, silencing our inner voices, and considering our feelings unimportant. We have become so accustomed to "pushing through" life's challenges that we've forgotten to pause, reflect, and respond thoughtfully.

Self-nurturance encourages us to rediscover this vital practice. It involves tuning into the gentle whispers of your soul and responding with compassion rather than judgment. This means being aware when you feel depleted and allowing yourself the time to replenish. Most importantly, it involves being present for yourself during both the good times and the challenging times.

Self-nurturance is unique to each individual. For some, it might mean finding solace in quiet moments of reflection or meditation. For others, it could involve setting boundaries to protect their peace, finding joy in creative expression, reconnecting with nature, or simply allowing themselves to rest.

There is no universal formula or one-size-fits-all approach. Self-nurturance involves discovering what genuinely nurtures your mind, body, and soul and honoring those needs in an authentic manner. It requires curiosity to explore, patience to learn, and a willingness to adapt as you discover what works best for you.

Self-nurturance emphasizes the mindful act of engaging with oneself, pausing to listen, respect, and nurture oneself as tenderly as one would for others.

It requires continuous introspection and the courage to act on that understanding.

Self-Nurturance vs. Self-Care

You might be wondering: Isn't self-nurturance simply another term for self-care?

In some ways, they are alike. Both emphasize prioritizing your wellbeing and acknowledging the importance of replenishing your energy.

However, while self-care often centers on specific activities, self-nurturance encompasses broader and deeper aspects.

Self-nurturance isn't just about what you do; it's about how you show up for yourself. It's the spirit of kindness and empathy that you bring with you every day, reflected in how you speak to yourself during moments of struggle, the grace you extend to yourself when things don't go as planned, and the commitment you make to your growth and healing.

In other words, self-care can be a component of self-nurturance, but self-nurturance includes so much more. It is a mindset and a way of living that affirms I am worthy of love, care, and attention—not just from others but from myself.

Self-nurturance encourages you to look past mere self-care checklists and cultivate a lasting bond with yourself. It involves maintaining an inner sense of support and validation as you move through life, making your wellbeing a core aspect rather than an occasional concern.

Why It Matters

In my work, I often meet individuals who are physically, emotionally, and mentally exhausted. They feel overwhelmed by life's demands and unsure about how to nurture themselves amidst it all.

Though they come for answers, strategies, or solutions,

they often uncover something more profound: the need to reconnect with themselves.

As a professional who works with individuals on their journeys of healing and growth, I have witnessed the transformative power of self-nurturance. It is neither a magic cure nor a quick fix; it is a foundation.

It is crucial as it helps you reconnect with yourself and serves as a reminder that you are more than your responsibilities, achievements, and the roles you play in the lives of others. It enables you to return to your center, where your strength, resilience, and sense of purpose reside.

Practicing self-nurturance creates a foundation for emotional wellbeing. It equips you with the resources to face life's challenges without compromising your 'Self.'

You become more aware of your needs, gain confidence in setting boundaries, and improve your ability to cultivate meaningful relationships. You begin to engage with the world not from a place of emptiness but from a place of abundance.

Self-nurturance builds resilience- not the kind that comes from gritting your teeth and pushing through, but the type that enables you to bend without breaking. It helps you create an inner sanctuary, a safe and strong place you can return to, no matter what challenges arise.

Most importantly, it's an expression of self-love. It affirms your worth, not because of what you do but because of who you are.

By nurturing yourself, you transform your life and become better equipped to support the people and causes that matter to you, as it's not just a gift to yourself but also the world around you.

The Role of Self-Nurturance in Emotional Wellbeing and Resilience

Picture yourself constructing a home. The foundation is crucial for the house's strength. It enhances stability during storms and supplies the necessary structure for creating something enduring. Without a robust foundation, even the most stunning home may collapse under pressure.

Similarly, self-nurturance serves as the foundation of our emotional wellbeing and resilience. Without it, we become unstable and susceptible to life's pressures.

However, when we dedicate time to nurture ourselves, we fortify that foundation, empowering us to withstand life's unavoidable challenges. It's fundamentally an act of love directed inward, a space often overlooked.

Many of us feel compelled to evaluate our value by the extent to what we offer to others, whether it's through caring for our families, supporting friends, or pursuing success. While these endeavors are admirable, there is a crucial truth: you cannot sustain your efforts in an empty tank. By replenishing yourself mentally, physically, and emotionally, you generate the energy and resilience needed to sustain yourself. With this renewed energy, you can better support the people and commitments that matter most to you.

The Importance in Emotional Wellbeing

Our emotions resemble rivers; they continually flow, change, and adjust to life's ups and downs. However, ignoring self-nurturance is like allowing debris to accumulate in those rivers. Stress, resentment, and burnout can obstruct that flow. Soon enough, everything feels stagnant, leaving us overwhelmed, exhausted, and disconnected from ourselves.

Prioritizing self-nurturance is like clearing a riverbed. It requires removing obstructions to allow our emotions to flow freely once again. By doing so, we create space for positive feelings of joy, appreciation, and calm to enter, rekindling the experience of truly being alive.

Self-nurturance allows us to experience emotions without judgment. It grants us the space to fully embrace whatever we're feeling, whether it's bright and cheerful like a sunny day or intense and overwhelming like a storm.

Rather than suppressing or ignoring our feelings, self-nurturance encourages us to approach those emotions with compassion. This kind of self-compassion is fundamental to emotional wellbeing. It enables us to process our experiences, release burdens, and advance with greater ease and clarity. By taking the time to nurture ourselves, we accomplish more than simply navigating life's challenges; we further empower ourselves.

The Importance in Building Resilience

Life is undeniably beautiful, but it presents us with challenges. We encounter heartbreak, loss, setbacks, and unexpected turns that can derail us.

Resilience doesn't stem from evading tough times. It arises from how we nurture ourselves during and after such experiences.

Consider resilience like a muscle, with self-nurturance serving as the essential rest and recovery it requires to develop. Without this, we risk overextending ourselves, operating on empty until we have nothing to offer.

By dedicating time to self-nurturance, we cultivate an

inner reservoir of strength, a profound source we can rely on during tough times.

It doesn't need to involve anything extravagant or demanding. It could be as simple as setting boundaries to safeguard your energy, allowing yourself to rest when fatigued, or speaking kindly to yourself when you falter. These small, mindful actions accumulate over time. They form a safety net that supports you in moments of difficulty and cushions the effects of life's unavoidable hurdles.

Resilience is frequently depicted as toughness and grit. However, genuine resilience is about adaptability, like a willow tree that bends gracefully in the wind. It involves recognizing when to pause, breathe, and heal before moving forward.

Self-nurturance allows you to be human, embracing both your vulnerabilities and strengths simultaneously. It encourages you to embrace your softer side.

Resilience means giving yourself time to rebuild and grow so that you rise again with a more open heart.

A Lighthouse in the Storm

Envision being lost at sea, with waves crashing around you, the horizon obscured, and no land in sight. Then, you spot a lighthouse in the distance, its constant beam piercing through the turmoil and leading you back to safety.

This lighthouse represents self-nurturance. While it doesn't eliminate the storm, it offers you direction. It reassures you that, despite the chaos, there is always a route back to calmness, security, and your true self.

In overwhelming times, self-nurturance serves as our anchor. It's present in those quiet moments when we pause to breathe deeply, in the comforting rituals that calm our hearts, and in the soothing inner voice reassuring us, *"You'll be alright."* Although seemingly minor, these moments help us reconnect with our inner strength, the kind that requires no external recognition. It is consistent and stabilizing, much like the earth's pulse beneath us.

Self-nurturance serves as a guiding light that helps us remember our true selves, even amidst the fiercest storms. It propels us onward, one steady step at a time, until we regain our footing on solid ground.

The Promise of Self-Nurturance

Embracing self-nurturance allows you not only to meet your emotional needs but also to redefine the story you tell about your worth. You affirm, *"I am worthy of love, kindness, and wholeness."*

As this belief strengthens, a remarkable transformation occurs: you become better prepared to confront life's obstacles with grace, courage, and a renewed sense of purpose.

Start now. Take a moment to pause, listen, and show yourself kindness, just as you would to someone you truly care about.

Remember, you, too, deserve it!

Each small act of self-nurturance brings you closer to the emotional freedom and resilience you deserve. It isn't merely about surviving life; it's about flourishing with a heart that feels fulfilled and a spirit that feels empowered.

CHAPTER 2

LACK OF SELF-NURTURANCE: IMPACT ON SELF AND OTHERS

The Withering Garden

Imagine walking through a once-lush, vibrant garden. The flowers that once bloomed in vivid colors now appear withered. The soil, once nourishing and fertile, is now dehydrated from neglect. Weeds have crept in, choking the life out of what was once a thriving and beautiful space.

The gardener isn't absent; he is there, working tirelessly. However, his efforts are directed elsewhere. He is tending to his neighbor's garden, pulling weeds, watering plants down the road, and lending tools to anyone who asks.

In his selfless care for others, he has forgotten the most crucial garden of all: his own!

This is precisely the outcome when we overlook our own needs. As we invest our energy into our families, friends, jobs, and responsibilities, we gradually disconnect from the foundation of our wellbeing. Our emotional roots grow fragile, excitement wanes, and a relentless, overpowering fatigue replaces joy.

The most troubling aspect is that we often fail to notice it happening until we are completely drained.

Neglecting self-nurturance affects not only ourselves; it also extends outward, influencing all facets of our lives. It alters our presence in relationships, our pursuit of life goals, and our worldview.

A lack of self-nurturance often appears as a subtle neglect of one's physical and emotional needs. This can be reflected in various aspects of our lives and sometimes goes unnoticed because it often hides behind busy schedules, selflessness, or the pressure to meet expectations.

Let's explore what this lack of self-nurturance looks like and how we can transition from neglect to nurturing, ensuring that the 'individual' who requires us the most-ourselves- is never overlooked again.

The Common Signs of Lack of Self-Nurturance

A lack of self-nurturance often infiltrates our lives quietly, masking itself as busyness, productivity, or selflessness. It doesn't always announce its presence loudly, but its effects become apparent in subtle yet significant ways. Here's how it might manifest:

Being Constantly Busy

You are always on the go, taking care of others or handling endless to-do lists, having little to no time for yourself. Even when you have a moment to relax, you feel guilty or unproductive, and you keep pushing forward.

Ignoring Basic Requirements

Basic rituals of self-nurturance, such as eating nutritious

meals, drinking enough water, and getting sufficient sleep, often become a low priority. You skip meals, stay awake to fulfil your commitments, dismiss signs of fatigue, telling yourself there is no time to rest.

Emotional Overload or Disconnection

You feel overwhelmed by emotions like anxiety, frustration, irritability, helplessness, and sadness, or you feel completely numb and disconnected. It becomes hard to process your feelings or understand why you are struggling.

Lacking self-nurturance makes it difficult to manage emotions healthily, resulting in them being repressed or erupting at unpredictable times.

Self-Criticism and Perfectionism

Your inner dialogue is harsh and unforgiving, criticizing every mistake while demanding constant perfection. You continually push yourself to accomplish more, improve, or reach impossibly high standards, allowing no space for self-compassion or acceptance.

Lack of Boundaries

Constantly saying "yes" to others becomes the norm, even when it drains you. You feel obligated to meet everyone else's needs, often at your own expense, and find it difficult to establish healthy boundaries to protect your energy.

Loss of Joy

The activities you once enjoyed that brought you happiness now seem like distant memories or insignificant. Hobbies, interests, and even relationships have lost their excitement. Life feels more like an endless series of commitments and obligations, rather than something meaningful and fulfilling.

Constant Fatigue and Tension

You constantly feel tired and worn out, and the idea of resting seems like a distant wish that remains just out of reach. Gradually, this weariness seeps into every aspect of your life, making even basic tasks feel daunting.

Your body begins to exhibit tension through symptoms such as headaches, acid reflux, frequent colds, muscle spasms, sleep disturbances, overeating, or loss of appetite. If you keep ignoring your needs, this neglect could lead to more serious health issues in the long run.

Struggling with Challenges

When we lack the inner strength that self-nurturance provides, even the smallest setbacks can feel pretty daunting. It can make it trickier to manage stress, adapt to changes, or recover from challenges.

Feelings of Resentment or Unappreciation

You may feel unappreciated or overlooked as if others fail to notice or value the things you do. This feeling of resentment can accumulate over time, resulting in frustration or strained relationships.

Lack of Self-Nurturance doesn't happen overnight; it's usually a gradual drift from the nurturance, attention, and time we owe ourselves. Identifying these indicators isn't about criticism; it's focused on awareness. Once you understand how this deficiency impacts you, you can begin taking steps to restore your wellbeing.

Lack of Self-Nurturance: Impact on 'Self'

Imagine being a candle shining brightly in a dark space. Your light offers warmth and comfort to others, guiding them on their path. However, with each flicker, your wax diminishes, and your flame drains the very essence that fuels it. If you never take a moment to refill, what happens? The light fades. Eventually, it extinguishes.

This is the experience of living without self-nurturance. You continuously give until there's nothing remaining—not for others and certainly not for yourself. Emotional exhaustion creeps in, often going unnoticed initially, yet its influence permeates every aspect of your life. You may find yourself snapping at loved ones over trivial matters, feeling bitterness when agreeing to another obligation, or collapsing at day's end feeling empty, as if you've emptied every ounce of energy without anything to show for it.

Disconnecting from Your Inner Self

Ignoring self-nurturance not only depletes your energy but also distances you from your true self.

Your needs and your happiness begin to feel unimportant and slowly fade into the background. Instead, your attention becomes outwardly focused, you are always busy fulfilling the needs, expectations, and demands of others.

Over time, you might feel as though you've lost touch

with your own reflection in the mirror. The individual reflected back seems unfamiliar, someone whose needs and wishes have been overshadowed by the burden of always giving.

This disconnection doesn't occur suddenly.

It is like a boat that has slowly come loose from its anchorage, drifting away over time. Eventually, you wake up to find that you no longer recognize who you've become.

The passions that once set your soul ablaze have faded, overshadowed by a continuous cycle of obligations and external demands.

The Effects on the Body

Your body excels at signaling when something is amiss, but those signals often go unnoticed without self-nurturance. Stress lingers in the background, showing up as sleeplessness, migraines, or chronic stress and exhaustion. You may experience unexplained aches and pains or notice that you're falling ill more frequently as your immune system struggles to cope.

Your body sends these warning signs, saying, "Something is off. Please pay attention!"

However, instead of noticing these signals, we often brush them off as a normal part of life. We persist, pushing through as if exhaustion and discomfort are marks of 'being strong'. Over time, this exhausting cycle takes a toll on us, making us vulnerable both emotionally and physically.

Emotional Impact of Neglect

Living without self-nurturance alters your emotional landscape. What once brought joy or fulfilment now feels burdensome, like a chore. Frustration and resentment seep in, obscuring your interactions and making it difficult to engage with others authentically. You might feel depleted, like a well that has run dry, leaving no reserves to offer.

Worse still, you might begin to internalize these emotions, mistaking them for an indication of your worth. "Why can't I manage this? Why am I always exhausted?" The reality is that this isn't about your value or ability; it's about the foundational nurture you've overlooked. Without self-nurturance, even the most resilient among us will ultimately feel the strain.

Identifying the Pattern

The cycle of neglect is subtle, but it can be disrupted. The initial step is to identify how you're depleted—recognizing the impact it has on your mind, body, and spirit. Needing nurturance is not a weakness; it's a fundamental aspect of being human. The earlier you respect that need, the sooner you can replenish your energy, reignite your passion, and reconnect with yourself.

Lack of Self-Nurturance: Impact on 'Others'

The Leaky Bucket

If you've ever tried to carry a bucket with a hole in it, you understand the frustration it brings. Regardless of how much water you pour in, it keeps leaking out. This is precisely what happens when you try to assist others while you're depleted. You try to provide support endlessly without fixing your own bucket, but you're actually left with nothing to offer others.

Impact on Relationships

Neglecting self-nurturance affects not only us but also the important people in our lives. Even minor daily interactions can feel too demanding when our emotional energy is low. Even a small request for assistance from a partner may seem burdensome, while a child's desire for attention can feel overwhelming. This doesn't mean we love them less; rather, we are so exhausted that we lack the ability to engage with patience, kindness, or presence.

We may find ourselves snapping at family members, pulling away from relationships, or feeling irritated by their needs. This guilt and frustration create a damaging cycle. We genuinely want to support those we care about, but without nurturing ourselves, we cannot engage fully with them.

Impact on Children

For parents and caregivers, the stakes are even greater. Children act as mirrors; they reflect your actions. If they see you continually putting yourself last, failing to set boundaries, and ignoring your own needs, they are likely to adopt these behaviors. They may grow up viewing self-sacrifice as virtuous and self-nurturance as selfish.

Impact on the Workplace

Neglecting self-nurturance affects you beyond your homes and seeps into your jobs. Burnout becomes an invisible burden, diminishing both your productivity and enthusiasm for work. Operating on fumes results in waning creativity, replaced by feelings of obligation or dread. Consequently, errors increase, and interactions with coworkers may deteriorate.

Lacking the resilience fostered by self-nurturance, even small setbacks can seem overwhelming. Deadlines become sources of anxiety, constructive feedback is perceived as criticism, and the satisfaction of achievement gives way to mere relief that a task is completed. Over time, this pattern not only negatively impacts our productivity but also erodes our sense of purpose and fulfilment in our work.

A key advantage is that this cycle can be interrupted. By prioritizing self-nurturance, we begin to repair the leaks in our bucket. This restores our emotional reserves, enabling us to give from a place of abundance rather than scarcity. The change is remarkable. We become more patient, more present, and better equipped to tackle life's challenges with greater ease and grace.

We present our best selves in our relationships, demonstrating how to balance caring for others with self-nurturance. At work, we replenish our energy and creativity, discovering renewed purpose in what we do.

It starts with the simple yet transformative act of turning inward and checking in on oneself. When you prioritize self-nurturance, the positive impacts extend to every area of your life and everyone around you.

CHAPTER 3

SELF-NURTURANCE: THE SURROUNDING MYTHS AND FACTS

Nurturing yourself is not selfish, its essential to your survival and your wellbeing – Renee Peterson Trudeau

When we nurture something or someone, it is often viewed as a selfless act that deserves admiration and praise. Many philosophies emphasize the importance of prioritizing care for others, seeing it as the foundation of a virtuous life.

Then, why is self-nurturance often seen as self-centered or indulgent? Why isn't it acknowledged everywhere as a necessity?

Let's examine the myths surrounding self-nurturance and uncover the truths we need to accept in order to reclaim it.

Self-Nurturance: Contradictions and Doubts

Have you ever found yourself at the edge of a tranquil forest trail, ready to follow a path designed just for you, only to hear that familiar inner voice whispering, "Shouldn't you be doing something more meaningful? Isn't this selfish? What will others think?"

That voice, the relentless critic that appears when you try to nurture yourself, represents self-doubt. It is as if every move you make toward self-nurturance is accompanied by an invisible string, dragging you back and making you question your worthiness of this journey.

But why does this happen? Why does something so essential to our emotional and physical wellbeing feel unsettling, almost forbidden?

The answer lies deep within us, hidden in the stories we have been told, the roles we have been trained to play, and the beliefs we have absorbed about what it means to be a "good" person.

The Unspoken Scripts We Carry

Visualize your mind as a vast library filled with volumes you didn't choose to write. These volumes contain the untold stories of your life, narratives shaped by your upbringing, culture, and society.

Among those pages, you may discover a chapter titled: "Putting yourself first is selfish" or "Your worth is determined by how much you contribute to others."

For years, you have read and re-read that chapter, accepting it as truth.

Now, as you start to rewrite your narrative, softly saying, "I deserve to nurture myself too," it feels a bit strange. It's as if you're violating unspoken rules in a game you hadn't known you were participating in.

From a young age, you are often taught to prioritize others, whether it's family, friends, or various other responsibilities, and to place them above yourself. You begin to associate sacrifice with love, busyness with achievement, and selflessness with moral integrity.

While there is undeniable beauty in generosity, this viewpoint provides little opportunity for the giver to pause, relax, and nurture their own soul.

So, when we finally attempt self-nurturance, that internal voice of doubt rises, asking, "Are you sure you are allowed to do this?"

The Fear of "Not Enough"

At its core, self-doubt about self-nurturance often stems from a deep-seated fear of inadequacy: the feeling of not being enough, not doing enough, or not giving enough. It is the constant worry that by choosing yourself, even for a brief moment, you are somehow failing in your responsibilities to others.

Imagine being a juggler, constantly managing a dozen balls: work, family, relationships, errands, and commitments. When you finally take a moment to breathe and set down just one ball to tend to yourself, self-doubt surfaces like a strict supervisor, murmuring, "What if everything crumbles because you paused? What if you drop all the balls?"

But here's the truth: you aren't a juggler; you're a human being.

Just as a painter steps back to appreciate their canvas and a musician embraces silence to compose a symphony, you must also take pauses. These moments are essential for nurturing yourself and sustaining the life you are diligently crafting.

Self-Nurturance Vs. The "Selfish" Label

A common myth we encounter frequently is that self-nurturance is selfish. The term "Self" often makes us feel uneasy, implying that looking inward inherently means neglecting others. Let's take a closer look at this belief.

Nurturing ourselves helps restore our energy, enabling us to be fully present for the people and things we value.

Self-nurturance isn't exclusionary; instead, it's a form of preparation that ensures we have the ability to give without exhausting ourselves in the process.

Nurturing ourselves doesn't mean we're proclaiming, "I am more important than others!" Instead, it conveys a deeper, simpler message: *"I matter too."*

Valuing ourselves can often lead to discomfort because we have been taught to see self-nurturance as either indulgent or wasteful. We live in a culture that celebrates productivity, sacrifice, and the constant need to meet others' expectations.

Taking a moment to prioritize our own needs can feel like straying from the norm, as if we are challenging the principles we've learned.

For the longest time, self-nurturance was often seen as an act of rebellion. It is viewed as a subtle defiance against the prevailing notion that we must constantly give, do, and be more for others. Such rebellion, regardless of how minuscule, often evokes feelings of doubt.

However, the reality is this: your worth isn't defined by your doubt. It is simply a part of the stories you have encountered, stories that can and must be redefined.

By embracing self-nurturance, you not only grant yourself the right to flourish but also set an example for others that valuing yourself is perfectly acceptable.

The Shadow of Comparison

Another factor contributing to self-doubt in self-nurturance is the shadow of comparison. You observe others seemingly juggling everything with ease, excelling in their careers, caring for their families, and achieving their goals.

You then question yourself, "If they can manage without taking a break, why can't I?"

This question stems from self-criticism and creates a false sense of inadequacy. You set unattainable standards for yourself, comparing your internal struggles to the flawless facade others display in the world.

The reality is this: what appears on the surface is never the full story. You never get to know the sacrifices they make, the personal struggles they endure, and the quiet exhaustion they bear. The actual cost of their accomplishments remains unseen, as does the potential compromise to their wellbeing.

The comparison paints a distorted image, highlighting only the successes and achievements while sidelining the underlying nuances, complexities, and challenges people face.

Consider this: the growth of a sunflower compared to that of a pine tree. Both thrive, but they grow in distinct ways, under varying conditions, and at different speeds. A sunflower quickly blooms, stretching toward the sun with vibrant colors. In contrast, a pine tree gradually increases in height, firmly anchored in the soil while developing resilience over time. Neither is superior nor inferior; they simply represent different growth patterns.

This applies to us, too. Your journey to self-nurturance may differ from that of others, and that's perfectly fine. What truly matters is respecting your needs, rhythm, and unique journey.

When you feel the urge to compare yourself to others, remember this: your worth isn't determined by how tirelessly you work. Thriving isn't about exhausting yourself to meet an unrealistic standard. It's about knowing when to pause, take a break, prioritize your wellbeing, and allow yourself to grow into the person you are meant to be.

The Pressure to Always Be "Doing"

Our society consistently emphasizes the need for constant action. Productivity is viewed as a badge of honor, while rest is frequently seen as laziness. We are overwhelmed by messages that associate self-worth with accomplishments: the more you achieve, the more valuable you appear.

In this environment of relentless hustle, prioritizing self-nurturance can feel like defying societal norms and resisting what is often overly valued.

But here lies the irony: *the more you focus exclusively on doing, the more you become detached from being.*

It is through being that we rediscover balance, clarity, and a deeper sense of self. If life is a journey, then our 'doing' is the path we follow, while our state of 'being' serves as the compass that guides us. Without moments of reflection and stillness, we may lose sight of our true motivations. We start to move just for the sake of moving, confusing busyness with purpose and speed with genuine progress.

Taking time for self-nurturance does not mean abandoning others; rather, it enables you to engage with them more deeply and purposefully. You pause to refresh and regain clarity in your thoughts. These moments allow you to return to your duties, relationships, and interests with greater energy and clarity.

The world may glorify *doing*, but it's the integration of *being* that makes our efforts meaningful.

Self-nurturance is not an escape from life; it is a form of self-alignment that helps ensure your actions are driven by intention rather than fatigue.

Rewriting the Script

The journey toward the self begins with rewriting the narrative—the unspoken story that convinces you that self-nurturance is unacceptable.

Start by gently examining the roots of this belief. Inquire within: "Where did this notion originate? Who influenced me to think that nurturing for myself is selfish or inappropriate?"

You may find that many of your beliefs do not actually belong to you. Instead, they have been inherited from your family, culture, or society, much like a hand-me-down coat that doesn't quite fit. Perhaps you adopted the perspective of your caregivers who regarded sacrifice as the highest expression of love, or a culture that idolised constant productivity, or friends who equated busyness with worth. While these narratives may have benefited others, they do not have to dictate your life.

After recognizing these inherited narratives, remember this simple yet powerful truth: self-doubt isn't a stop sign. Rather, it indicates that you are entering new and unfamiliar territory.

Isn't that always the case for growth?

Recall your initial attempts to ride a bike—it was unsteady and perhaps a bit intimidating. You wobbled, stumbled, and fell, but over time and with determination, those initial awkward movements evolved into a natural habit.

This process is similar to self-nurturance. At first, it may seem strange or uncomfortable to prioritize your needs and create space for yourself. However, with consistent practice, it will evolve into a fundamental and natural rhythm in your life.

Start by making small, gentle adjustments to your script.

Rewriting the script doesn't mean erasing the past; rather, it involves intentionally choosing a new story that reflects your truth. This fresh narrative will gradually replace doubts and reservations with profound insight:

self-nurture is essential, not extravagant. By prioritizing your wellbeing, you embrace your responsibilities and duties with greater strength, clarity, and purpose.

Embracing Your Right to Nurture

Imagine standing before a mirror, looking into your eyes, and saying, *"I deserve this."* Not because you have checked off every item on your checklist or reached a specific milestone.

It's about celebrating your existence, the unique journey you're on, and the richness that comes from simply being alive.

Self-nurturance is your inherent right. It is not something to earn or to prove your worth; it is essential. Just like every living being needs nurturance to thrive, so do you.

Self-doubt may never completely disappear; it often lingers in the background, whispering, "Are you sure this is okay?" Shouldn't you be achieving more?"

You don't have to allow it to dictate your decisions. You

can acknowledge this voice, recognize it, and then let it go. Much like a passing cloud in a vast sky, it doesn't have to lessen your self-worth.

Let self-nurturance be your foundation, a consistent practice reminding you of your identity, intrinsic value, humanity, and entitlement to thrive. Putting yourself first is a courageous act, an understated yet powerful declaration.

Something extraordinary happens when you nurture that belief and move beyond your doubts to embrace the 'Self fully'. You not only transform your own life but also impact the lives of those around you. You inspire others to follow your example. Your commitment to honoring your needs generates waves of strength, resilience, and inspiration that reach far beyond yourself.

So, the next time self-doubt whispers, "Shouldn't you be doing something else?" pause, take a breath, and smile.

Then, respond calmly, *"Yes, I am doing something else. I am nurturing myself."*

Because you deserve this not for what you do but for who

you are!

A Personal Responsibility to Oneself

Have you ever looked at a tree and thought it to be self-centered for soaking up the sunlight? Or seen a river flowing and blamed it for being self-serving as it collects fresh rain?

Certainly not!

Nature needs self-nurturance to flourish. Trees require sunlight, water, and soil as nutrients to grow tall, withstand wind, and provide shade. Similarly, rivers depend on rain to flow, sustain their journey, and nurture life.

By nurturing yourself, you replenish your energy and strength while building your capacity to give more freely and fully. Just as a healthy tree provides shade and a flowing river sustains life, you can only be there for others when you feel nurtured, grounded, and whole.

Think about it: When you feel depleted, how does it

affect your presence? You may become irritable, unfocused, or too tired to engage fully.

Alternatively, when you are well-rested, emotionally fulfilled, and in tune with yourself, you present with clarity, patience, and openness. The energy you radiate extends outward, impacting everyone around you.

As Lord Krishna says in the Bhagavad Gita, "One who is balanced in eating, sleeping, working, and recreation achieves yoga, which destroys all suffering."

This balance is not an indulgence; it is an alignment. Neglecting our own needs disrupts this harmony, making it harder to fulfil our roles in life.

Self-nurturance is a sacred responsibility. When we nurture ourselves, we replenish the energy that fuels our ability to serve, love, and contribute to the world.

Right to Respect and Love 'Self'

Have you ever thought about the type of love and nurturance you seek from others? It might be gentle kindness during your toughest moments, supportive words when you're feeling lost, or simply the feeling of being recognized, valued, and understood.

Now, think about this: Are you offering that same love and nurturance to yourself?

As humans, you need nurturance, attention, and affection, not only from others but also from yourself. This is as fundamental as the air you breathe or the water you drink. Still, due to cultural conditioning, societal pressures, or personal insecurities, you often hold back from nurturing yourself in the way you wish to get from others.

The reality is that the love you give to yourself is just as important as the love you receive from others, perhaps even more so. This is an act of self-respect, a statement that your needs and feelings are valid, demonstrating that you deserve them simply by being yourself.

Treating yourself with compassion meets essential physiological and psychological needs. Ignoring the self can lead to feelings of depletion, including burnout, disconnection, and a persistent sense of emptiness. It's similar to trying to quench your thirst from a well that has long run dry.

Self-nurturance is the bridge that reconnects you to yourself.

As ancient wisdom suggests: *"Atmanam vidhi"- Know thyself.*

Self-respect begins with self-awareness, which in turn fosters self-nurturance. Like a seed that needs sunlight and water to thrive, your soul requires love and nurture to blossom. The affection you extend to yourself establishes the basis for all the love you can share with others.

When you seek external empathy, validation, or encouragement, know that you can and must provide it for yourself. Show yourself the same respect and compassion you would extend to someone you truly care about.

Self-nurturance is not just an act of self-respect; it is a powerful way to reclaim your worth, completeness, and the love you have always been worthy of.

Foundation of a Fulfilling Life

Self-nurturance forms the foundation for your emotional and psychological wellbeing. It provides the stability and strength needed to build a life that not only looks good on the outside but is also whole and fulfilling on the inside.

Neglecting your needs is like living with a hole in your heart. This neglect leads to sickness, hopelessness, sadness, and emptiness; no external love or achievements can replace the self-nurture that you owe to yourself.

Genuine fulfillment stems not from external achievements or material wealth but from inner harmony. By nurturing yourself, you cultivate a sense of harmony, allowing your inner self to remain stable amidst the storms of your external environment.

Nurturing the 'Self' is a Generous Act

Let's redefine self-nurturance as what it really

represents: an act of generosity that not only supports your own wellbeing but also generates waves of positivity that affect those around you.

It focuses on the importance of giving rather than receiving, ensuring that you possess the energy, clarity, and strength to keep supporting the people and causes that are important to you. This exemplifies leading a balanced and mindful life.

Allow your light to shine brightly as a generous gift to those who accompany you on your journey.

Cannot Pour from an Empty Cup

Imagine standing under the blazing sun, holding a cup of cool water to quench your thirst in the heat. As friends and family approach asking for sips, you pour out some, wishing to help. But soon, the cup runs dry. Now, you stand thirsty and drained, with nothing left to give.

This illustrates what happens when you neglect self-nurturance. Giving endlessly without replenishing depletes your energy and ability to nurture. You may push through for a while, but eventually, you hit a wall with nothing to offer.

Now imagine this: instead of emptying your cup, you pause to refill it. You refill your water and then share it with everyone else.

Something changes!

By addressing your needs, you not only quench your thirst but also gain the strength and energy to support others. This is what self-nurturance is - taking time to rest, reflect, and care for yourself enhances your ability to give meaningfully.

If you ever feel guilty for prioritizing self-nurturance, remember your cup.

Refill your cup as an act of wisdom and love.

Self-nurturance ensures your giving is abundant and sustainable, starting with receiving the care you deserve.

Leading by Example

When you embrace self-nurturance, you're not only caring for yourself; you're also conveying a powerful, unspoken message to everyone around you. This simple yet profound act can inspire those who look to you for guidance—your children, friends, employees, or anyone who admires the way you live your life.

Whenever you focus on your own needs, you set a good example. You demonstrate the importance of balance, show that establishing boundaries reflects respect, and affirm that self-nurturance is a way to honour your own existence.

Children learn more from our actions than our words. When they notice you setting boundaries, saying no to excessive demands, and prioritizing your own rest and rejuvenation, they will come to realize that nurturing themselves is really important.

This principle applies to all areas of life, including the workplace, home, and community; your actions have far-reaching effects.

Practicing self-nurturance demonstrates that caring for yourself enhances what you give. A rested and balanced person contributes more than a drained one.

Embracing self-nurturance creates a healthier circle of influence, modelling a lifestyle that values self-respect and balance, inspiring others to follow suit.

Prioritizing wellbeing paves the way for others, demonstrating that self-nurturance is essential for a joyful and meaningful life.

Coping with Frustration and Exhaustion

Let's be honest; giving endlessly without ever pausing to nurture yourself can feel like pouring water into a bottomless well. At first, you may do it willingly, even joyfully, but as the demands pile up and your energy begins to dwindle, a quiet voice inside starts to whisper, "Why doesn't anyone see how much I'm sacrificing?"

And that's when frustration begins to creep in…

The joy of helping others is replaced by exhaustion and

bitterness. Instead of strengthening relationships, it can strain them, turning it into a heavy obligation. No one wants to give out of guilt; we wish to offer from the heart, with sincere care and connection.

This is where self-nurturance changes everything…

When you take the time to meet your own needs first, you break the cycle of depletion and resentment. Instead of giving because you *'have to'*, you give because you *'want to'*.

Your kindness feels lighter, freer, and more sincere because it flows from a place of abundance, not emptiness.

And here's the most beautiful part: self-nurturance not only benefits you; it also preserves the beauty and harmony of your relationships. You ensure that your connections with others are based on love, mutual respect, and authenticity, not quiet frustration and hidden exhaustion.

Connect with the Authentic Self

When you nurture yourself, you reconnect with your true and authentic self. It's like clearing dust from a neglected mirror, allowing you to see your genuine reflection more clearly. Your passions, values, and distinctive strengths, all those elements that define you, re-emerge into focus.

This connection subtly and powerfully guides you toward what truly matters. It allows you to navigate life with clarity and intention rather than feeling pressured by the endless demands, distractions, and chaos of the present. Self-nurturance not only rejuvenates you; it also realigns you, helping you return to your core.

You engage in relationships attentively, work with focus, and participate in the community authentically. Your energy flows steadily like a river, quietly strengthening those around you.

Imagine the ripple effect of this connection. Your grounded energy can comfort a friend, encourage a colleague, or bring peace to your family.

An Expression of Love

Fundamentally, self-nurturance embodies love, the love for the world you influence.

Imagine a world where everyone embraces self-nurturance, navigating life with balance, purpose, and connection. Wouldn't such a world be more harmonious and loving?

Self-nurturance contributes to a more compassionate and interconnected world. By prioritizing yourself, you help create an environment where empathy and understanding thrive, allowing love and harmony to flourish.

This practice honors not only your existence but also the lives you impact, the relationships you cultivate, and the world you're shaping.

Enhances Efficiency and Innovation

Have you ever noticed how everything flows more smoothly when you feel your best?

With a clear mind, steady energy, and an uplifted spirit, tasks that once felt overwhelming become manageable, even enjoyable. This doesn't happen by chance; self-nurturance boosts both efficiency and innovation. Allowing yourself time for rest, reflection, or a little joy sharpens your focus, sparks creativity, and reveals your potential.

Self-nurturance isn't just about feeling good; it creates conditions for clarity, intentional action, and inspired results.

Reflect on the relationship between rest and inspiration. Many of history's greatest ideas, ranging from scientific innovations to works of art, arise not during periods of excessive labor but rather in moments of rest and contemplation. By nurturing yourself, you cultivate the mental environment necessary for ideas to flourish and solutions to come to light.

Next time you feel stuck, uninspired, or overwhelmed, take a moment and ask: "What do I need to feel refreshed and focused?" Whether it's a break, a walk, or a quiet moment of stillness, remember that these acts of self-nurturance do not detract from your work; they enhance your effectiveness, creativity, and ability to present your best self.

By fueling your efficiency and innovation with nurture, you're not just getting things done; you're doing them with intention, excellence, and a sense of fulfilment.

Maintains Emotional Composure

Making room for self-nurturance significantly changes your life, enabling you to face challenges with composure and poise.

You become like a tree in a storm: firmly rooted, resilient, and flexible enough to sway without breaking. Even when life's winds howl, your inner stability keeps you grounded, enabling you to face challenges with strength.

This emotional composure is not just a gift for yourself; it's a gift for everyone else. When you are centered, your interactions with others become more seamless and empathetic. Conversations flow more smoothly, and potential conflicts lose their intensity. Your calm demeanor creates a positive atmosphere, fostering understanding, patience, and harmony among those around you.

Nurturing your emotional wellbeing enhances your life and positively impacts your surroundings. It may be a family member who feels secure in your composure, a colleague who appreciates your thoughtful approach, or a friend who finds comfort in your presence—your inner equilibrium significantly influences those around you.

Learn to Draw and Honor Limits

Self-nurturance gently teaches you to recognize and respect your own limits. It shows that boundaries aren't barriers to excluding others; they act as bridges that facilitate balanced, meaningful, and healthy connections. It doesn't mean saying no to others but saying yes to yourself so that you can be fully present for them.

They signify, "I value my wellbeing, and because of that,

I can show up for you with greater presence, patience, and authenticity." Far from being selfish, boundaries create a framework in which care and connection can thrive.

Shift Your Perspective

Instead of asking, "Is self-nurturance selfish?" shift the question to, "How can I nurture myself so I can be my best self for others?" This simple change in perspective reframes self-nurturance from a source of guilt to an essential part of thriving. It helps you see self-nurturance for what it truly is: a gift, not just to yourself but to everyone you influence.

Recognizing self-nurturance as a fundamental aspect of a fulfilling and meaningful life reduces feelings of guilt. You come to realize that nurturing yourself is not an act of indulgence; rather, it is an expression of love that extends beyond yourself. This practice restores your energy, strengthens your resilience, and ensures that the kindness, patience, and care you offer others come from abundance rather than emptiness.

So, the next time you feel tempted to set your needs aside, remind yourself that self-nurturance is the foundation of a life well-lived and a love well-shared.

And remember this: *"You, just like anyone else, are deserving of that nurture. By honoring your needs, you honor your worth, your relationships, and the unique light you bring to the world."*

"Never be ashamed to say, 'I'm worn out. I've had enough. I need some time for myself.' That isn't being selfish. That isn't being weak. That's being human."
~Topher Kearby

CHAPTER 4

PATHWAYS TO SELF-NURTURANCE FOR WELLBEING AND RESILIENCE

Self-nurturance is uniquely personal to each individual. Just as no two people are alike, our methods of self-nurture also differ based on our unique needs, preferences, and life circumstances. Indian traditions offer subtle yet impactful insights highlighting how wellbeing is rooted in balance, harmony, and the capacity to nurture our inner selves.

Self-nurturance provides countless ways to cultivate resilience and maintain wellbeing, whether by embracing moments of stillness, engaging in mindful rituals, or connecting with nature. It's about listening to your inner voice and responding accordingly, whether this involves taking a moment for contemplation, engaging in activities like yoga or meditation, or simply allowing oneself to relax.

The concept of balance is deeply embedded in our perspective on life, whether it's the habits of the mind, the elements of the body, or the rhythms of the seasons. Self-nurturance involves aligning with that balance, allowing space for joy, inner strength, and clarity to flourish amidst life's demands.

This chapter will explore various ways to nurture your body, mind, and spirit. Ranging from simple daily routines to profound changes in your life approach, every path offers a chance to deepen your connection to yourself and cultivate a harmonious, resilient life.

Self-nurturance goes beyond mere self-care; it involves building a foundation that enables you to give, grow, and flourish. Together, let's explore these paths, uncovering practices that align with your heart and promote your wellbeing in the most natural and fulfilling manner.

Various Pathways to Self-Nurturance...

Extravagant actions or strict habits don't define self-nurturance; it revolves around identifying what genuinely feeds your body, mind, and spirit. It involves listening to yourself with kindness and curiosity, seeking practices that align with your inner desires, and incorporating them into your daily routine in ways that feel organic and uplifting.

The joy of self-nurturance stems from its adaptability. There isn't just one correct approach to this. Rather, numerous paths exist, small yet significant practices that resonate with your values, tastes, and individual life pace. These routes can be as easy as taking a mindful breath, enjoying a brief moment of calm, or engaging in a meaningful conversation. Alternatively, they may encompass stronger commitments such as establishing daily routines, developing new habits, or rekindling old passions.

In this section, we invite you to explore these modes of self-nurturance with an open heart. Consider this a gentle invitation to reconnect with yourself, uncover the paths that bring joy, balance, and resilience, and discover the ones that truly resonate with you.

You may find comfort in the peaceful stillness of

meditation, energy in the rhythm of movement, or tranquility in nature's embrace. You might discover the power of journaling your thoughts, expressing your creativity, or acknowledging your need for rest. Whichever path you choose, remember that every step leads to a deeper, more vibrant connection with yourself.

As you embark on this journey, remember that self-nurturance is not about achieving perfection; it's about being present. It's about offering yourself the gift of self-nurture and meeting yourself exactly where you are, one gentle step at a time.

Let's explore these pathways together and discover what nurtures you and helps you thrive.

Physical Self-Nurturance: Tuning Your Instrument

Think of your body as the instrument that lets you craft the melody of life. When was the last time you really paused to listen to its tune?

In Indian tradition, the body is regarded as a sacred

vessel—'*Deham Devalayam*'—a temple that houses the spirit. Tuning it begins with the fundamentals: nourishing meals, adequate hydration, and restorative sleep. However, it doesn't stop there. Just as a sitar must be meticulously tuned to produce its finest sound, your body flourishes through intentional care and balance.

Gentle movements such as yoga, morning walks, or even dancing to your favorite tune can help reset your body and mind.

Make this journey personal by embracing methods that resonate with you, gently reassuring your body that it is loved and truly valued.

Let physical self-nurturance be your way of tuning your body's temple so it plays life's melody with clarity, balance, and joy.

Recommended Practices:

- **Morning Stretch to Start the Day**

Picture waking up and reaching for the sky with a gentle

stretch, feeling your muscles come alive to greet a new day. Practice basic Surya Namaskar (Sun Salutation) or neck and shoulder rolls while still in your pyjamas.

It serves as a "refresh" button for your body, preparing it for the day ahead.

- **Short Breaks In Between**

Set a gentle reminder every few hours for a 5-minute stretching break. While seated at your desk, try spinal twists or wrist rolls, or stand up and stretch your arms overhead as if reaching for the clouds.

These brief breaks help energize your body and sharpen your focus.

- **Outdoor Walking**

A brief stroll outdoors, whether in a local park or around your neighborhood, can rejuvenate both your body and mind.

Walking barefoot on grass, also known as earthing, further enhances your reconnection with nature and offers a sense of grounding.

- **Nutritious and Healthy Meals**

Imagine blending a colorful and vibrant smoothie, where each sip feels like a nourishing hug for your body, or enjoying a comforting bowl of khichdi. This not only energizes you but also satisfies your taste buds.

It gently reminds you to treat your body with kindness and care and provides the essential nutrients and warmth you need.

- **Conscious Eating**

Set aside one meal each day for mindful eating. Take small bites, savor the flavors and textures, and pay attention to the aromas.

Whether it's chapati with sabzi or a simple bowl of lentil soup, treat your meal as a moment of thankfulness for the nourishment it provides.

- **Personalized Nurturing Approach**

End your day with a calming ritual that honors both your body and mind. Light up the space with soothing light, and listen to relaxing music.

Take a moment to reflect on the nurturing you're providing, acknowledging it as an expression of love and self-respect.

Emotional Self-Nurturance: Replenishing Your Inner Reservoir

Your emotions resemble water in a reservoir. When they are balanced and replenished, they provide energy, flow, and vitality to your life. Emotional self-nurturance involves filling this reservoir, enabling you to face life's challenges with strength and grace.

Acknowledge your feelings without judgment. Similar to the concept of *"Sakshi Bhava,"* or witness consciousness, in Indian philosophy, observe your emotions as they arise without labeling them as good or bad.

Journaling serves as an effective outlet; write down your thoughts and feelings unfiltered, allowing yourself the freedom to express what lies within fully.

Remember that emotional self-nurturance also involves protecting your energy reservoir. Setting boundaries and saying no when necessary are not selfish actions; they are acts of self-nurturance that enable your emotional energy to replenish rather than deplete.

Nurturing your emotional wellbeing fosters inner balance and flow, allowing you to maintain your quality of life while extending patience, kindness, and understanding to others.

Recommended Practices:

- **Daily Check-In**

Take a moment, once or twice a day, to identify and accept your feelings without any judgment. Close your eyes, breathe deeply a few times, and quietly ask yourself, "What am I feeling right now?"

This simple practice can help you reconnect with your inner emotional landscape.

- **Documenting Thoughts and Feelings**

Keep a small notebook or diary to document your thoughts and feelings. Write with prompts such as, "I felt frustrated today when…" or "I experienced joy when…"

Delve into the reasons behind your feelings as though you're engaging in a frank dialogue with yourself.

You might also want to use an exclusive pen or notepad to emphasize the purpose and significance of this practice.

- **Self-Compassion Notes**

When you're feeling down, write a kind note to yourself, just like a caring friend would. Open with warmth, saying, "I see you. I understand this is tough, but you're doing your best."

Reading it out loud can provide additional comfort.

- **Media as a Comfort Refuge**

On difficult days, curl up with an uplifting movie or a relaxing playlist. Enjoy an inspiring classic film or a selection of soothing ragas to lift your spirits.

Media provides a comforting escape into stories and experiences that resonate with our lives.

Pair this with a cozy blanket and warm food or drink to form your own emotional sanctuary.

- **A Box of Joy**

Decorate a box and fill it with items that evoke joy or peace, such as a small souvenir, a meaningful letter to yourself, a cherished photo, or a small token of spiritual solace.

Opening it feels like unwrapping a thoughtful gift from your former self.

- **Appreciation and Gratitude**

Each day, jot down three things you're grateful for. It can be something as simple as the warmth of the morning sun, the joy of laughter, or a nice cup of chai enjoyed with a loved one.

This habit subtly redirects your attention to life's

positives, enriching your emotional reservoir with hope and gratitude.

Mental Self-Nurturance: Nurturing Your Inner Explorer

Like a curious explorer, your mind flourishes with healthy stimulation, curiosity, and rest. It continually seeks to learn, organize, and innovate. Nurturing your mind means offering this explorer enriching experiences while also allowing time for quiet reflection, integration, and rejuvenation. It brings clarity, creativity, and insight.

Like a well-tended garden, a cultivated mind provides fertile ground for ideas, solutions, and inspirations that enrich every aspect of your life.

Recommended Practices:

- **Reading Time**

Dedicate 10 to 15 minutes each day to read inspiring,

thought-provoking, or challenging materials. This can be a novel, biography, or a captivating article.

Consider this time as an opportunity to explore new ideas and perspectives.

- **Exploring New Genres**

Select a film, music, or book from a genre you haven't yet explored. You might want to delve into historical fiction focused on ancient civilizations or classics or explore a poetry collection that highlights a rich literary tradition.

Stepping outside your typical choices sparks your imagination and expands your perspective.

- **Brain Work**

Dedicate 10 minutes each day to a joy-inducing puzzle, such as sudoku, crossword puzzles, or a classic chess challenge.

Imagine that gratifying "aha" moment as you solve a challenging problem, sharpening your mental acuity.

- **Continued Learning**

Commit to learning something every day. It can be as simple as a single Sanskrit phrase, the name of a prominent historical figure, or an intriguing trivia fact about art or culture.

These small discoveries nurture your intellectual curiosity.

- **Upgrade Yourself**

Sign up for a course to explore subjects you've always wanted to learn, such as digital photography, cooking, painting, or traditional arts and crafts.

Imagine using your new skills to capture breathtaking sunset photos or create artwork for your space, experiencing the confidence and joy that comes with it.

- **Practice Mindfulness**

Spend some time practicing mindfulness meditation or deep breathing. Focus on your breath or repeat a calming, positive mantra.

These peaceful moments can help clear your mind, promoting a sense of calm and clarity.

Spiritual Self-Nurturance: Igniting the Inner Candle

Within each of us lies an inner candle that symbolizes peace, purpose, and a connection to something greater than ourselves. Spiritual self-nurturance means caring for this flame, ensuring it remains steady and bright, even in the face of life's inevitable challenges.

Explore activities that nurture a deep connection, whether with yourself, others, or the universe. This may include prayer, meditation, or chanting a sacred verse. Alternatively, some might discover a connection through nature walks, stargazing, or practicing gratefulness. Each of these experiences allows you to connect with the sacred and nourish your inner light.

By nurturing your spirit, you affirm, *"I am more than just what I accomplish."* You choose to honor the journey of seeking, connecting, and simply existing. By doing so, you ensure that your inner light shines brightly, illuminating your path and that of those around you.

Recommended Practices:

* **Meditation and Breathwork**

Find a quiet spot, close your eyes, and focus on your breathing. Take a deep breath, feeling the cool air fill your lungs, then exhale gently, releasing any tension.

Just five minutes of this practice can feel like hitting pause on life's chaos. You might also include a simple positive verse to enhance your serenity.

* **Connecting with Nature**

Take a walk in a park, forest, or along the beach, paying attention to the rustling leaves, birdsong, and calming waves. Feel the ground beneath your feet and the breeze on your skin.

This practice serves as a gentle reminder of your connection to nature and its rhythms.

- **Cultivating a Grateful Mindset**

Before bedtime, take a moment to reflect on what you are grateful for today. This might include simple things like a warm meal, a kind word, a compliment, a supportive family member, a colleague, a smile from a child, or the beauty of a sunset.

Let gratefulness and positivity serve as your life's anchor.

- **Contemplative Reflection**

Take a moment to reflect on some thought-provoking questions like, *"What do I need to let go of?"* or *"What am I seeking in this moment of my life?"*

Writing down your thoughts can help bring clarity and serve as an excellent tool for deeper self-exploration.

Creative Self-Nurturance: Letting Your Colors Shine

Creativity is how your soul colors the world with its distinctive shades. It is a celebration of self-expression, a realm where your imagination runs free and your inner world comes alive.

Creative self-nurturance encourages you to let your colors shine without fear or judgment. It isn't centered on achieving perfection; it's about expressing yourself and finding happiness in the journey of creating something that resonates with you- a true reflection of your inner light. Embrace your colors; they are as boundless as your imagination.

Recommended Practices:

- **Sketching and Doodling**

Keep a small notebook or sketchpad handy to doodle when inspiration strikes. Create simple patterns, mandalas, or any whimsical designs.

Remember, it is not about creating a masterpiece; it's about letting your creativity flow freely.

- **Reorganizing the Space**

Transform a corner of your home into a creative retreat by arranging your books, introducing a vibrant color, or showcasing a beloved piece of art or a painting.

Such minor adjustments can rejuvenate your outlook and spark fresh ideas.

- **DIY Vision Board**

Collect old magazines, scissors, and glue to make a vision board. Trim images and words that represent your goals, dreams, or the atmosphere you want to create. Add symbolic features, such as nature images, spiritual symbols, or something that elevates your mood.

Watch your ambitions come to life on a vibrant, personalized board.

- **Discover Various Mediums**

Explore a new creative medium just for enjoyment. Try pottery, explore traditional cooking, pen some poetry, or design jewelry.

Keep in mind that the delight is in the journey of exploration rather than the quest for perfection.

Social Self-Nurturance: Strengthening Connections

Relationships resemble bridges: elegant and enduring when strong, yet they demand consistent care and attention to support their weight. Social self-nurturance strengthens these bridges through affection, consideration, and respect.

Nurture relationships that uplift and inspire you. Spend time with those who fill your heart with joy and calm your spirit. It's equally important to ensure that your end of the bridge is sturdy.

Healthy communication, openness to vulnerability, and the courage to ask for support are essential components that strengthen these bonds. Additionally, establishing boundaries is a vital part of nurturing your social wellbeing. Boundaries safeguard your emotional energy, ensuring that your relationships remain sources of happiness and support rather than stress or tension.

Social self-nurturance involves both giving and receiving. Embrace the love, care, and kindness that others want to share with you. By nurturing your relationships with intention and balance, you build bridges that are strong and lasting, enhancing your life and the lives of those around you.

Recommended Practices:

- **Connection Check-Ins**

Connect with at least one person each week, whether by call, message or in person. A simple inquiry, such as "How have you been?" or sharing a meaningful moment from your day, can spark a heartfelt conversation.

- **Reaching Out to Friends**

Reach out to an old friend with a warm message, like "Hey, I was just thinking about our trip to the mountains! How have you been?"

Reignite your connection by reminiscing about the fond memories that bring back great times for both you and them to bond.

• Quality Time

Set aside uninterrupted time for your loved ones. Enjoy a meal, a cup of chai, or a walk together. Spending quality time and being genuinely present strengthens your connection, creating joyful and meaningful memories.

• Meetings Your People

Plan a Sunday brunch or tea date with a close friend or family member. Imagine laughing, reminiscing, enjoying each other's company, and leaving with a sense of lightness and a deeper connection.

These shared experiences weave the golden threads of your relationships.

• Engaging with Community

Join a local book club, yoga class, or hobby workshop. Connecting with others who share your interests can bring joy to your social life and help you form new friendships.

Explore cultural or creative groups to deepen these connections.

- **Establish Boundaries**

Learn to say 'No' to requests or commitments that drain your energy. Establish "quiet times" and inform others of your unavailability; this might include turning off notifications or finding a quiet spot with a book.

Healthy boundaries protect your energy and ensure that your relationships remain supportive instead of exhausting.

Empathetic Self-Nurturance: Being Compassionate to Yourself

Being empathetic toward yourself means nurturing your inner self, allowing you to see yourself not as a series of flaws but as a complete, beautiful, and evolving individual.

Imagine talking to yourself as if you were speaking to a dear friend. Pay attention to your approach, choice of words, tone, and body language to understand if you are showing the same compassion to yourself as you would to your loved ones.

Practicing self-compassion doesn't mean disregarding your imperfections; instead, it involves embracing them with kindness and empathy.

It's important to recognize that being human means being flawed, and that's perfectly okay.

You are deserving—just as you are.

Recommended Practices:

- **Acknowledge Your Efforts**

Write a simple note to yourself: "Dear Me, I admire how you managed [specific challenge]." Fold the note and place it in your journal, wallet, or beneath your pillow.

When you revisit this physical reminder of your inner strength, it will inspire you and strengthen your resilience.

- **Affirmation Notes**

Post affirming notes, such as "You are enough" or "You are doing your best," on your bathroom mirror, bedside table, or desk.

Each time you see them, it serves as a gentle reminder to be kind to yourself, akin to a mantra you recite throughout the day.

- **Compassionate Reflection**

When feeling overwhelmed, pause for a moment to sit in silence. Place your hand gently on your chest, close your eyes, and repeat, *"It's alright to struggle. I'm here for me."*

Imagine enveloping yourself in a warm, soothing hug, as if you are lovingly embracing your inner self with care and compassion.

Environmental Self-Nurturance: Crafting Your Sanctuary

Picture a lively little garden on your balcony, brimming with colorful flowers and thriving plants. Just imagining it can lift your spirits, enhance your positivity, and create a sense of connection. The environment we inhabit significantly influences our emotions and state of mind. Environmental self-nurturance involves turning your space into a sanctuary, a manifestation of your inner tranquility and happiness.

Cultivating a peaceful environment isn't about achieving perfection; it's about intention. It involves creating an environment where you can unwind, rejuvenate, and reconnect with yourself. By nurturing your environment, you enhance your wellbeing, transforming your home or workspace into a sanctuary that echoes your inner peace and resilience.

Recommended Practices:

- **Declutter with Intention**

Select a drawer, shelf, or space, and carefully evaluate its contents. Ask yourself, "Does this item bring joy or fulfil a purpose?" Donate or recycle items that no longer resonate with your life, creating space for clarity and peace.

- **Arrange Your Corner**

Pick a spot or corner in your room, whether it's a bedside table, a desk, or a shelf, and organize it.

Include a meaningful item, such as a framed photo or a positive quote, to transform it into a haven of peace and positivity.

- **Bring Nature to Your Space**

Introduce nature into your home with a low-maintenance plant, such as a money plant or a small Tulsi pot. While watering it, consider it a symbol of your personal growth and resilience.

Place natural items, such as stones, seashells, or fresh flowers, nearby for a calming and grounding effect.

- **Create a Cozy Retreat**

Arrange a chair by a window or in a peaceful corner, and set a small table nearby to hold tea or books. This becomes your cherished sanctuary of peace, perfect for reading or contemplation.

- **Bedtime Routine**

Take five minutes each night to organize your space. Fold clothes, tidy your desk, or adjust a cushion.

This simple task prepares you for a refreshing start in the morning, allowing you to awaken to a feeling of order and calmness.

Self-Nurturance: An Evolving Journey

Self-nurturance is an evolving journey, a continuous dance of care, growth, and self-discovery. Each path presents a unique rhythm that guides you towards balance and resilience.

Some days it resembles a grand symphony, vibrant and energetic; other days, it turns into a soft hum, a tranquil connection with yourself. Both experiences are valid and beautiful.

Which key will you choose today? Which path resonates with you most in this moment?

Tune in to your inner voice and allow it to guide you toward the self-nurturance your heart and soul yearn for right now. Every step you take honors yourself, your worth, your dreams, and your wellbeing.

That, above all, is a journey worth celebrating!

CHAPTER 5

THE TRANSFORMATIVE POWER OF SELF-NURTURANCE

For Aarav (Name changed), life centered on deadlines. As a successful architect, he excelled at solving problems, producing flawless work, and surpassing expectations.

However, a change occurred over the years. His previously inspired sketches now appeared robotic, his evenings were filled with fatigue, and the enthusiasm that once ignited his creativity seemed to fade away.

One day, while cleaning out an old storage cabinet, Aarav discovered a dusty sketchbook from his college years. Flipping through its pages, he noticed bold lines, vibrant ideas, and raw yet sincere creations. A small note written in the margin grabbed his attention: "Dream big. Draw for the joy of it." He paused, experiencing a nameless ache that lingered.

That evening, for the first time in years, Aarav picked up a pencil without any agenda. There were no client briefs, no deadlines—just an open page. Initially, his hand wavered, and the first few strokes felt clumsy. Yet, as time passed, he felt a shift within himself. He started to sketch not for validation but for his own enjoyment.

This simple gesture unlocked new possibilities. Aarav began to carve out small moments for himself, taking morning walks to refresh his mind, preparing meals that evoked memories of his childhood, and even turning down projects that didn't align with his values.

As time passed, Aarav observed subtle yet significant transformations. His designs evolved into bolder expressions, infused with a creativity he had long overlooked. Conversations with colleagues became more engaging as he interacted with them genuinely rather than under pressure. Most importantly, he felt revitalized, as if the life he had been constructing was now one he truly desired to experience.

Self-nurturance was not about a dramatic change in

Aarav's life; it involved a series of intentional, small decisions. Yet, these choices rejuvenated him, reigniting his creativity, energy, and sense of purpose.

This chapter focuses on those choices—minor yet impactful ways that self-nurturance can transform our lives. It emphasizes that nurturing yourself is not merely a break from life's pressures but rather a proactive approach to living with intention, joy, and authenticity.

Self-nurturance serves as a significant catalyst for transformation. When you nurture yourself, you spark a chain reaction that influences every aspect of your life. It is like planting a seed in fertile soil; with consistent care, it thrives and transforms both itself and its surroundings.

This chapter explores how self-nurturance promotes change, affecting not only your inner self but also your perceptions of the world, your relationships, and your sense of purpose. Initially, these shifts might be subtle - a brief moment of clarity, a flicker of confidence- but, as time passes, they evolve into significant growth and transformation.

Change does not come easily. It can disrupt your habits, beliefs, and perceptions. Here, self-nurturance provides the resilience necessary to accept these changes with grace. By acknowledging your needs, you build a base for personal growth, an environment where you can release what no longer benefits you and invite what promotes your wellbeing.

As we explore the transformation brought about by self-nurturance, we will discover how it reshapes our mindset, deepens our relationships, and guides us toward a life that feels more authentic and aligned. Let's delve into this transformative potential and explore how adopting self-nurturance can lead to significant and lasting change.

Nurturing Continuous Development

By regularly prioritizing self-nurturance, you establish a strong base for self-discovery and personal growth. It is like constructing a resilient nest for your spirit, a safe place to return repeatedly for rest, reflection, and rejuvenation. With this support, you can spread your wings, venture into new realms, and pursue a life that aligns with your innermost dreams with courage.

In essence, self-nurturance leads to a kinder, more vibrant existence where stress diminishes, inner wisdom shines through, and both body and mind feel lovingly nurtured. It is a journey of tenderly caring for yourself like a cherished garden, day by day, season by season, allowing your life to flourish in ways you may have only envisioned.

Self-nurturance is a transformative journey that enhances both your care and your connection to the world. By embracing self-nurturance, you will notice significant changes impacting every aspect of your life. These are the shifts that come along with nurturing yourself:

Improved Emotional Understanding

Mastery Over Stress

A Sense of Belongingness

Self-management

Emotional Regulation

Self-Expression

Mindset Shift

Increased Empathy

Balanced Wheel of Life

Positive Wellbeing

Design a Self-Growth Path

Tech-Life Balance

Be Fully Present

Social Connection

Improved Emotional Understanding

Self-nurturance creates a reflective environment, enabling you to connect with complex emotions and identify the subtle triggers that evoke them. As you begin this introspective journey, you gain deep insights into your feelings, refining your emotional awareness. This increased clarity not only helps you navigate your inner world more smoothly but also enhances your capacity to empathize with the emotions of others. As a result, it nurtures deeper, more compassionate relationships that connect on a profound level. It is like tuning into the soft whispers of your heart, guiding you toward a more genuine existence.

By embracing kindness towards yourself and recognizing both your achievements and shortcomings, you naturally extend that same warmth and understanding to those around you.

Recommended Practice:

Take just five minutes each day to express your emotions: *"Today I felt [emotion] because..."* This simple act can truly help you connect with yourself!

Write a heartening note to yourself: *"You are giving it your all, and that is enough."* Similarly, extend emotional understanding to others: *"I see the effort you've been putting in—thank you."*

Over time, you'll start to recognize patterns that offer insights into your emotional landscape and that of others.

Mastery Over Stress

By actively engaging in self-nurturance, you cultivate more effective and holistic strategies for managing stress, building resilience, and achieving a sense of balance even in the face of adversity. Engaging in self-nurturance practices equips you with valuable tools to manage stress, allowing you to respond thoughtfully and calmly instead of succumbing to impulsive reactions. This intentional approach promotes a deeper awareness of your emotions, allowing you to navigate challenging situations with more ease and composure.

Recommended Practice:

When stress hits, practice box breathing: inhale for four seconds, hold for four seconds, exhale for four seconds, and hold again for four seconds. Repeat this process until you feel calm.

A Sense of Belongingness

Self-nurturing practices strengthen your bond with both your surroundings and your inner self, fostering a deeper sense of inner security and a more meaningful connection to the world around you.

As your sense of belonging strengthens, you become more attuned to your surroundings, allowing you to experience a richer, more gratifying relationship with the people and places that shape your world.

In essence, self-nurturance creates a harmonious cycle of personal growth and community engagement, enriching both your life and the lives of those around you.

Recommended Practice:

Consider joining a local club or group where you can actively contribute to the community, share interests with like-minded individuals, and build meaningful relationships. Being part of a community not only brings a sense of belonging but also allows you to grow personally.

Self-Management Skills

Self-nurturance empowers you to prioritize your needs and responsibilities with clarity, manage your time wisely, and maintain a strong focus on your goals. This creates a deeper sense of awareness and fulfilment, ultimately guiding you toward a more intentional and satisfying life.

By taking the time to nurture yourself, you develop the resilience and motivation necessary to face daily challenges and pursue your aspirations wholeheartedly.

Recommended Practice:

Start your day by identifying three key priorities and setting aside 15 minutes for self-nurturance. This routine allows you to care for yourself while fulfilling your responsibilities.

Emotional Regulation

You develop the ability to respond to emotions with measured calmness and clarity, effectively minimizing impulsive reactions. This practice not only fosters emotional stability but also enhances your overall emotional intelligence, enabling you to handle challenging situations with greater ease and composure.

Recommended Practice:

If you're feeling overwhelmed, pause for a moment and remind yourself, *"Feeling this way is perfectly natural."*

Self-Expression

Taking the time to nurture yourself boosts your confidence and deepens your understanding. This inner growth allows you to express your thoughts, needs, and desires more clearly and effectively, developing more authentic connections with others and creating an environment where your voice is heard and valued.

Recommended Practice:

Engage in self-expression by writing, drawing, or discussing your feelings openly with a trusted friend.

Mindset Shift

Self-nurturance cultivates a mindset deeply rooted in personal growth, empowering you to meet challenges and seize opportunities with a sense of positivity and an open heart.

By prioritizing your wellbeing and personal growth, you create an environment that fosters resilience and curiosity, enabling you to navigate life's twists and turns with enthusiasm and grace.

This approach not only enhances your ability to navigate difficulties but also enriches your overall experience, fostering a deeper connection with yourself and the world around you.

Recommended Practice:

Transform negative thoughts into positive ones.

For example, instead of saying, "I failed," say, *"This experience taught me something valuable."*

Increased Empathy

Taking the time to nurture yourself not only replenishes your soul but also enhances your ability to empathize with and connect deeply with others. This fosters an understanding of their feelings and experiences, ultimately strengthening bonds and enriching your interactions.

Recommended Practice:

When someone shares their struggles, listen without offering advice. Just acknowledge their feelings by saying, *"I hear you, and I'm here for you."*

A Balanced Wheel of Life

Self-nurturance brings a sense of harmony and balance across the diverse facets of life, weaving together the threads of career, relationships, health, and personal growth. It helps to create a more fulfilling and enriched existence.

In embracing self-nurturance, you discover the

interconnectedness of these life areas, leading to a more vibrant and harmonious life experience.

Recommended Practice:

Assess your life using a wheel of life exercise. Select one area that seems overlooked and commit to a brief daily practice to enhance it, such as a quick physical workout for physical health or maintaining a journal for mental wellbeing.

Positive Wellbeing

Engaging in consistent, small acts of kindness significantly improves your mental, emotional, and physical wellbeing. These intentional gestures, whether offering a compliment, lending a helping hand, or simply listening to someone in need, create ripples of positivity that help others and promote a profound sense of inner peace within yourself.

In essence, these daily acts serve as a powerful reminder of our shared humanity and the impact we can have on each other's lives, ultimately leading to a more fulfilling and positive wellbeing.

Recommended Practice:

Begin each day with a positive step, such as taking time to help someone in need, practicing yoga, or gardening before you dive into your daily routine.

Design a Self-Growth Path

Self-nurturance is a vital practice that empowers you to take charge of your personal journey. When you prioritize your wellbeing and growth, you build a strong foundation that helps align your actions with your goals and aspirations.

When you engage in self-nurturing activities whether it's setting aside time for reflection, pursuing hobbies that bring you joy, or cultivating positive relationships, you create a harmonious environment where your ambitions can flourish.

Ultimately, self-nurturance becomes a powerful catalyst

that propels you toward your dreams, bringing a deeper sense of fulfilment and purpose along the way.

Recommended Practice:

Create a vision board filled with images and words that reflect your dreams and aspirations. Use it as a daily reminder of your journey.

Tech-Life Balance

Establishing clear boundaries around the use of technology can help you reclaim valuable time for engaging in offline activities that nourish your soul and enhance your overall wellbeing.

By intentionally limiting screen time and digital distractions, you create space for activities that bring you joy and fulfilment, such as reading, spending time in nature, or connecting with loved ones.

This mindful approach not only helps reduce the stress and anxiety associated with constant connectivity but also brings a more balanced and fulfilling life to you.

Recommended Practice:

Create a "tech-free" zone in your home, such as the dining table or bedroom, and set designated "tech-free" hours to enforce a daily screen time limit.

Be Fully Present

Engaging in self-nurturance improves your ability to be fully present in your day-to-day life, allowing you to immerse yourself in the moment. This practice enhances your appreciation of life's experiences, leading to a more meaningful engagement with the world around you.

This heightened awareness allows you to entirely engage in the moment, appreciating the richness of life's experiences.

Recommended Practice:

Engage in mindful eating by paying attention to the flavor, texture, and aroma of your food. This one simple practice keeps you anchored in the present moment.

Social Connection

Taking the time to nurture yourself can strengthen your connections with others and positively influence your community. You contribute better towards a shared sense of belonging among individuals in your surroundings, making it a more vibrant and inclusive place for everyone

Recommended Practice:

Set aside time each week to nurture a relationship, whether through a sincere message, meeting for coffee, or volunteering for a meaningful cause.

When you regularly nurture yourself, you create a subtle yet powerful effect that transforms your life experiences, emotions, and relationships with others. These small acts gradually evolve into significant inner transformations.

CHAPTER *6*

DO- IT- YOURSELF SELF- NURTURANCE PRACTICES

"Be there for others, but never leave yourself behind." –
Dodinsky

Self-nurturance goes beyond habit; it represents a profound respect for oneself!

When you nurture yourself, you honor your worth and create a ripple effect of positivity for everyone around you. Ignoring your own needs sends an unspoken message about how you value yourself; it is difficult to gain respect from others if you do not first respect yourself. You deserve the best, and that starts with how you treat yourself.

Nurturing yourself is among the most essential habits to develop. However, it's so easy to neglect your own needs, believing that other priorities should take precedence. This is a serious mistake, akin to attempting to craft a meaningful narrative with a dry pen. Replenishing your energy promotes a more vibrant life for yourself and those around you.

Nurturing Yourself: Caring for Your Inner Sanctuary

Self-nurturance practices function as essential instruments in your personal wellness toolkit. These practices empower you to take charge of your own wellbeing without relying on external support or professional help. They focus on nurturing your physical, emotional, mental, and spiritual health. Imagine each action as a drop of water that nourishes the seed of self-nurture, which eventually grows into a thriving garden of wellbeing.

As a mental health professional and life coach, I often see how daily pressures, self-doubt, and emotional burdens can weigh heavily on individuals, causing them to feel disconnected from themselves and the opportunities life presents. Many clients come to me looking for ways to ease anxiety, handle their stress, and move forward with a fresh sense of purpose. I've repeatedly found that true transformation doesn't result from drastic, sweeping changes; instead, it emerges from small, intentional acts of self-nurturance woven into daily routines. Self-nurturance is essential for mental health and emotional wellbeing. It involves a daily commitment to nurture yourself, allowing you to show up more powerfully, steadily, and resiliently in life. The strategies outlined below are designed to help you shift from merely surviving to achieving inner balance, confidence, and empowerment.

This chapter offers effective self-nurturance techniques, featuring daily practices aimed at managing stress, enhancing your mindset, and cultivating a life full of greater optimism, purpose, joy, clarity, and connections.

The Power of a Daily Routine: Cultivating Stability and Harmony

A well-organized daily routine provides stability, clarity,

and a sense of control. In chaotic times, having a routine serves as an anchor, helping to lower stress levels and boost productivity.

Begin your day with a regular morning routine—this could include stretching, sipping warm water, or practicing deep breathing for a few moments. Create a daily plan that includes work, self-nurturance, relaxation, and personal development activities. Conclude the day with reflection—consider a appreciation journal, listening to soothing music, or simply acknowledging what went well.

Tip: Establishing a regular routine helps in emotional regulation, reduces decision fatigue, and improves mental clarity.

Discipline: The Connection Between Goals and Reality

Discipline turns self-nurturance into a consistent practice rather than something pursued only when convenient. Without discipline, even the best intentions can fade away.

Start with a small step and commit to a daily self-nurturing practice, such as drinking water, stretching, reading, or deep breathing. Ensure accountability by tracking your progress in a journal or an app. Set fixed self-nurturance times in your schedule that you will not compromise on.

Tip: Self-discipline is not about restrictions; it's about choosing what is best for you, even when that choice is the most challenging one.

The Importance of Sleep and Relaxation for Clear Thinking

Sleep acts as your brain's natural reset mechanism. It influences mood, decision-making, and energy levels. Insufficient sleep contributes to anxiety, stress, and emotional instability.

Establish a bedtime routine by lowering the lights, steering clear of screens, and participating in soothing activities. Maintain regular sleep and wake times, including weekends. Consider deep breathing, meditation, or sipping herbal teas if you have trouble sleeping.

Tip: Quality sleep boosts emotional control, memory performance, and overall health.

Nurturing the Mind and Body with Nutritious Foods

Your diet influences your emotions. Foods rich in nutrients energize your brain, whereas processed foods may lead to mood fluctuations and fatigue.

Consume balanced meals by emphasizing whole foods, proteins, and healthy fats. Keep hydrated since water influences brain function, energy levels, and digestion. Steer clear of emotional eating; instead, engage in mindful eating by truly savoring each bite.

Tip: Consider food as nourishment, not a form of punishment. Your body flourishes with the proper nourishment.

The Strength of Social Bonds and Family Moments

Strong connections reduce stress, improve mental wellbeing, and create a sense of community.

Cherish family time; even short, meaningful conversations can strengthen bonds. Make space for valuable friendships—surround yourself with those who uplift and inspire you. If you feel lonely, think about joining a support group, a hobby class, or participating in a community event.

Tip: We humans are inherently drawn to connection. Nurturing relationships enriches life and strengthens emotional resilience.

Time in Nature for Emotional Renewal

Nature lowers stress hormones, soothes the mind, and boosts creativity.

Set aside 15 to 30 minutes daily for outdoor activities—whether it's walking, gardening, or simply relaxing under a tree.

Engage with nature by observing a sunrise or sunset to gain perspective and cultivate gratefulness.

Take up hiking, trekking, or mountain climbing to challenge your limits. Relax by the sea, enjoying the soothing sound of the waves. Discover wonder and quietude through birdwatching and stargazing.

Tip: Nature resets our emotions and reminds us of the immense vastness of life beyond daily worries.

Guard Your Energy: Avoid Negative Influences

Your mental and emotional wellbeing depends on the energy you allow in your life.

Minimize negativity, avoid toxic conversations, endless social media scrolling, and energy-draining surroundings.

Establish boundaries and decline when something doesn't resonate with your peace. Protect your mental space by spending time in uplifting and energizing places.

Tip: Energy is infectious. Be selective about who and what you allow into your time and mental space.

Broaden Your Perspectives: Learning, Growth, and Exploration

Personal growth brings joy to life and prevents stagnation. Explore a new skill or hobby, like painting, music, language learning, or taking an online course.

Step outside your comfort zone by travelling solo, engaging in public speaking, or signing up for a new activity. Set an annual challenge for yourself, focusing on areas like fitness, growth mindset, or creativity.

Tip: You grow by having the courage to venture into the unknown.

Exploring Spirituality and Purpose

Spirituality, whether religious, philosophical, or personal, offers guidance, peace, and a sense of connection to a higher presence.

Practice meditation to cultivate inner peace. Explore spiritual or philosophical writings that broaden your perspective.

Engage in charitable or community activities; helping others nourishes the soul.

Tip: A spiritual connection builds resilience, and a sense of inner peace.

Morning Grounding: Establish a Positive Outlook for Your Day

Anxiety often builds up as soon as we wake, fueled by our mental to-do lists and persistent worries. Taking a moment to center yourself at the beginning of the day can help prevent that overwhelming sensation as you start your tasks.

Before reaching for your phone, take three deep breaths and stretch your arms wide. Set a simple, positive intention for your day, such as *"I will take things one step at a time"* or *"I am capable and enough."*

If possible, dedicate five minutes to quiet reflection while enjoying your tea or watching the sunrise.

Tip: This simple action can reorganize your brain, allowing you to start the day with clarity instead of stress, thus reducing morning anxiety.

Emotional Check-Ins: Acknowledge Your Feelings

Suppressing emotions results in mental overload, potentially leading to stress and anxiety. Acknowledging your feelings, even for a moment, allows for healthier processing.

Pause once or twice daily to reflect: "What emotions am I experiencing at this moment?" If you find your feelings overwhelming, take a deep breath and reassure yourself, *"Feelings are temporary, and I can manage them."*

If possible, consider writing them down openly and without self-censorship.

Tip: Recognizing emotions reduces their intensity and helps restore your control over your mental and emotional wellbeing.

Stress Relief: Mental Body Scan

When stress and anxiety build up, the body holds onto tension. Gentle movement acts as an effective stress reliever and can quickly improve mood.

Conduct a quick body scan to identify areas of tension, like your jaw, shoulders, or back, and give those areas a thorough stretch.

Step outside for a five-minute walk, focusing on your surroundings rather than your worries. Play a favorite song and allow yourself to move; this could be stretching, swaying, or even dancing freely.

Tip: Your body and mind are interconnected. Simply moving can help release trapped emotions and dissipate mental fog.

Reframing Negative Thoughts: Restore Confidence

Negative self-talk traps you in cycles of self-doubt and fear. By learning to reframe these thoughts, you can restore confidence and tackle challenges with a growth mindset.

When a self-critical thought arises, such as "I'm failing," take a moment to question it. Ask yourself, "Is this thought entirely true? How else can I view this?"

Reframe it with kindness: instead of saying, "I'm not good enough," try saying, *"I am learning and evolving, and that is sufficient."* If a situation seems daunting, remind yourself, *"This moment is difficult, but it won't last forever."*

Tip: Our thoughts influence our emotions. By changing negative thought patterns, we can enhance our self-esteem and gradually lower anxiety levels.

Rest and Relaxation: Essential for Resilience

Rest often takes a back seat in a society that prioritizes

constant activity. However, essential rest is crucial for emotional resilience, effective decision-making, and overall wellbeing.

Create a dedicated relaxation space and give yourself at least 15 minutes each day to fully unwind, free from distractions. You can achieve this by reading, lying down, or sitting quietly.

Tip: Allowing yourself to rest without feeling guilty is among the most effective forms of self-nurturance.

Joy Pause: Key to a Fulfilling Life

Joy and pleasure should not be seen as mere rewards for productivity; they are crucial components of a fulfilling life. By consciously incorporating small joys into your daily routine, stress becomes easier to handle, making life feel more abundant.

Take a "joy pause" during the day—whether it's relishing a piece of chocolate, listening to the birds chirping outside, or watching the clouds drift by.

Start an appreciation practice: note one thing that made you smile each day.

Tip: Incorporating small joys into daily life counteracts stress and enhances emotional resilience.

Conscious Connection: Strengthening Relationships

Human connection serves as a cornerstone of mental wellbeing. Nurturing relationships offers emotional support and strengthens one's sense of belonging.

Reach out to a loved one just to check on them. Practice deep listening. Set boundaries where needed.

Tip: Meaningful connections don't need to be long or elaborate. A quick two-minute check-in can uplift your spirits and those of others.

Tiny Self-Nurturance Activities

Here are some guided exercises designed to help you implement these enjoyable self-nurturing practices for each activity. These prompts and steps will assist you in seamlessly integrating them into your daily routine…

Cloud-Watching Break

Set aside two minutes during your day, perhaps during a break or after lunch. Find your view by going outside or standing by a window where you can see the sky.

Observe the clouds and allow your eyes to follow their shapes and movements. Envision each one as a passing worry, drifting further away with each breath.

Reflect, take a deep breath, and remember, *"Just like the clouds, my thoughts can come and go."*

Reflection Point: How was your experience watching the clouds? Did it affect your mood or perspective?

Tea or Coffee Ritual

Select a time that aligns with your usual tea or coffee routine, such as morning, afternoon, or evening. Connect with your senses and feel the aroma, warmth, and texture of the mug in your hands.

Take your time and enjoy each sip, letting the taste linger on your palate. As you drink, repeat a calming affirmation, like, *"This is my moment to relax."*

End with gratefulness, and show appreciation for the peace you've created in this moment.

Reflection Point: How did savoring your drink enhance the experience compared to consuming it hastily?

Serenity Scribble

Collect your materials, ensuring a notepad and pen are within reach on your desk, nightstand, or in your bag. Select a moment, like when tension increases, and take a minute to doodle. Create patterns, shapes, or random words without overthinking.

Release your grip and pay attention to the pen sliding across the paper. Envision the tension melting away with every movement. Take a moment to notice if your shoulders or jaw feel more relaxed after the exercise.

Reflection Point: What was the feeling of scribbling? Did it provide relief or a sense of liberation?

Mirror Pep Talk

Stop briefly by a mirror; as you wash your hands or brush your hair, take a moment to glance at your reflection.

Be compassionate and say a positive or supportive phrase, either aloud or silently, such as *"You're doing great"* or *"I'm proud of you for showing up today."*

Smile at yourself; even a tiny smile can lift your mood. Carry it forward, allowing the encouragement to accompany you throughout your day.

Reflection Point: What was it like to express kindness toward yourself? Did it change your feelings or how you view yourself?

Breathing Bouquet

Take a moment of quiet to pause, close your eyes, and concentrate on your breathing. Inhale for a count of four, hold your breath for two counts and then exhale for four counts. Repeat this process three times.

Visualize inhaling calmness as if you are gathering a bouquet of flowers, and exhale stress like scattering petals in the wind. Notice the shift; engage your senses and pay attention to what your body feels.

Reflection Point: In what ways did the visualization improve your breathing practice? Did it leave you feeling more grounded afterwards?

Moment of Thankfulness

Select a time and create a daily routine, like before bed or after waking up. Identify a single thing you are thankful for, such as the warmth of your blanket, a kind remark, or the aroma of your morning coffee.

Express your appreciation by writing it down or speaking

it aloud. Allow yourself to feel this genuinely. Acknowledge with a smile and conclude the practice by sealing the moment of appreciation with a gentle smile.

Reflection Point: In what ways did concentrating on gratitude influence your mood or perspective throughout the day?

Gentle Shoulder Rotation

Take a moment and sit comfortably at your desk or on the couch while keeping your back straight.

Rotate your shoulders forward in a circular motion five times, then switch to moving them backwards five times. Imagine the tension melting away, like smoothly ironing out wrinkles from fabric.

Assess your body and observe if your neck, shoulders, or upper back feels more relaxed.

Reflection Point: In what ways did this quick movement affect your physical and mental state?

One-Minute Clean-Up

Select a small area, such as the corner of your desk or a shelf. Set a timer for one minute and clean only within that time.

Prioritize clarity, organize items neatly, dispose of trash, and clean the surface thoroughly. Step back to admire the order and notice how the tidy space makes you feel.

Reflection Point: Has organizing a small space helped clarify or ease your thoughts?

Nature's Whisper

Choose your moment and stand next to a plant or a window with a view of greenery.

Take a closer look and pay attention to the details: the leaves' texture, the stem's curve, and the way sunlight dances on the surface. Imagine the plant breathing alongside you, a quiet rhythm of life.

Recognize your growth and softly remind yourself, *"Just*

like this plant, I'm also growing."

Reflection Point: How has connecting with nature influenced your feelings? Did it promote a sense of grounding or calmness?

Pocket-Sized Celebration

After completing a task, take a moment to acknowledge your accomplishment, no matter how small. Celebrate your way by choosing a gesture, be it a fist pump, a smile, or a whispered, "I nailed it!"

Celebrate your victory and let the feeling of achievement surround you, even if just for a moment.

Proceed to the next step, leveraging the energy from your celebration to tackle the upcoming task with enthusiasm.

Reflection Point: In what ways did acknowledging a small achievement influence your motivation or confidence?

Final Reflection Exercise:

At the end of the week, reflect on which small self-nurturance activities felt the most impactful. Write them down:

1. What were the successful aspects and their reasons?

2. How did these practices make you feel during and after?

3. One or two activities you would like to include more frequently.

These activities aim to simplify self-nurturance, making it both accessible and impactful. Even small acts of nurturance can generate a wave of peace and happiness throughout your everyday life.

There is no one "right" way to nurture yourself. Self-nurturance is highly personal, and what benefits one person may not be effective for another.

It is a journey, not a destination. Each of these practices is a stepping stone toward building a life rooted in balance, resilience, and joy. Begin with small steps, maintain consistency, and select what truly speaks to you. Rather than treating self-nurturance as an added chore, weave it into your daily routine in ways that seem effortless.

Let it be a supportive influence that boosts your mental health, enhances your emotional wellbeing, and helps you navigate life with greater ease and confidence.

Which of these strategies will you begin with today?

CHAPTER 7

MAKE SELF-NURTURANCE SUSTAINABLE

"There are days I drop words of comfort on myself like falling leaves and remember that it is enough to be taken care of by myself."

~Brian Andreas

Self-nurturance is not just a fleeting moment of pampering; it is a lifelong commitment to honoring yourself.

It's about recognizing your value and offering yourself the kindness and attention you need. Incorporating self-nurturance into your daily life conveys a strong message to yourself and those around you: your wellbeing is important.

This chapter acts as your guide to incorporating self-nurturance into your daily routine, ensuring it remains a sustainable practice despite life's challenges.

The Importance of Sustainability

In peaceful times, self-nurturance comes naturally. However, during stressful periods or when we feel pressed for time, it often gets overlooked, resulting in a cycle of neglect followed by recovery. Addressing this ongoing issue requires a strong emphasis on sustainability.

Self-nurturance is often viewed as a mere emergency measure, a means to recover only after experiencing burnout. In contrast, practicing sustainable self-nurturance helps level the ups and downs, providing consistent care instead of occasional relief. Consider it as consistently watering a plant rather than letting it dry out before watering it again.

Regular self-nurturance creates a strong foundation for both emotional and physical health. When confronted with life's challenges, this solid base helps you stay balanced, effectively manage obstacles, and recover more quickly.

The Importance of Daily Practices

Sustainable self-nurturance doesn't require major life changes or indulgences. Practicing small, regular acts of kindness for your body, soul, mind, and emotions daily is crucial. By incorporating these practices into your routines and tailoring them to your energy levels, celebrating even the smallest victories, and establishing clear boundaries for your wellbeing, self-nurturance becomes a vital, nourishing aspect of your identity.

These daily practices create a gentle, steady rhythm in your life, radiating affection and calm that sustain your joy and keep you aligned with what truly matters. Over time, self-nurturance will not just be something you engage in; it will evolve into the vibrant, sustaining rhythm of how you live.

Ensuring sustainable self-nurturance is an ongoing journey. Here's how to incorporate it into your life sustainably:

Sustainable Self-Nurturance: A Commitment to Life

Self-nurturance is a commitment to prioritizing your wellbeing and helping you face challenges with resilience. Let's understand how recognizing its importance promotes personal growth and emotional stability, leading to a more fulfilling life:

From Crisis to Preventive Self-Nurturance

People often engage in self-nurturance mainly when they feel stressed or exhausted. Effective self-nurturing involves looking after yourself before reaching that stage.

Change your perspective and consider self-nurturance as fuel, rather than just a repair tool.

Requirement Driven

Sustainable self-nurturance isn't a universally applicable approach; it should align with your lifestyle, personality, and needs.

It's about adaptability, not perfection. As your needs evolve, your self-nurturance should adjust accordingly.

Choose Kindness, Not Perfection

Many individuals struggle to practice sustainable self-nurturing, often feeling guilty for taking time for themselves or believing they must "earn" their rest.

This perfectionist mindset leads to burnout cycles, prompting them to neglect themselves when under pressure.

The kinder you are to yourself, the easier it becomes to sustain consistent self-nurturance.

Incorporate into Daily Life

Self-nurturance doesn't have to be separate from your responsibilities; it can be integrated into your daily routine without requiring additional time or effort.

The focus should be on incorporating self-nurturance into the time you already have rather than trying to find additional time for it.

Balance Independence and Support

Self-nurturance involves caring for oneself, but it doesn't mean handling everything alone. Sustainable wellbeing includes nurturing healthy relationships and creating community connections.

We flourish by being self-reliant while also connecting with a nurturing and supportive community.

Shield Your Energy

Toxic relationships, excessive social media use, and

negative self-talk can deplete your emotional energy. To nurture yourself sustainably, it's essential to safeguard your energy actively.

Energy management holds equal importance to time management; where you direct your energy impacts your overall wellbeing.

Embrace Fun, Imagination, Exploration

Many adults abandon playfulness and exploration, considering them unproductive. However, sustainable self-nurturance involves making space for joy, creativity, and fun, as they are essential to emotional nourishment and growth, not a diversion from it.

Align with Core Values

When self-nurturance aligns with your core values and purpose, it becomes more meaningful and sustainable.

It means choosing actions that align with the life you

want to build.

Sustainable Self-Nurturance and the Significance of "Quotients"

Let's explore how each of these qualities —emotional, humane, spiritual, empathy, sensitivity, compassion, kindness, listening, and non-judgment—serves as a guiding force that influences how we nurture ourselves and relate to others.

Emotional Quotient (EQ): Managing Emotions

Emotional quotient refers to the ability to understand, manage, and effectively handle emotions. Having a high EQ enables individuals to recognize their emotional needs, proactively address stress, and develop positive self-nurturing habits.

When experiencing emotional distress, a person with a high emotional quotient takes a moment to pause, reflect on their feelings, and adopt a balanced, mindful approach instead of reacting impulsively.

Humane Quotient (HQ): Treating with Dignity

Humane quotient emphasizes the importance of respecting the dignity of every individual, including your own. Individuals with high HQ engage in self-respect, self-acceptance, and self-kindness, which are key components of lasting self-nurturance.

Rather than blaming for a mistake, an individual with high HQ would gently remind themselves that imperfection is a part of the human experience.

Spiritual Quotient (SQ): Uncovering Purpose and Peace

The spiritual quotient refers to the capacity to connect with profound meaning, purpose, and inner peace. Nurturing spiritual wellbeing promotes resilience, a sense of appreciation, and lasting emotional stability.

In difficult times, a person with high SQ relies on faith, philosophy, or introspection to sustain emotional stability.

Empathy Quotient (EmQ): Recognizing the Needs

Empathy involves not only understanding the feelings of others but also acknowledging your own emotions, needs, and limitations. Individuals who possess a strong sense of empathy effectively balance supporting others with self-nurturance.

Rather than dismissing fatigue, a person with high EmQ would value rest and renewal, understanding that they cannot give from an empty cup.

Sensitivity Quotient (SeQ): Honoring Feelings

Individuals with a high sensitivity quotient feel emotions, energies, and their surroundings more intensely. This heightened sensitivity can become a valuable asset for self-awareness and self-nurturance when managed well.

A person with high SQ safeguards their emotional wellbeing by distancing themselves from negativity and engaging in soothing, nurturing activities.

Compassion Quotient (CQ): Exhibiting Gentleness

The compassion quotient enables people to address their challenges with warmth and gentleness instead of self-criticism. This is essential for enduring emotional resilience.

A person with high CQ responds to failure with compassion and a focus on growth rather than self-blame.

Kindness Quotient (KiQ): Nurturing Self-Kindness

Self-nurturance flourishes in an atmosphere filled with kindness, calmness, and patience. Individuals with a high Kindness Quotient (KiQ) prioritize being kind to themselves, enabling them to offer genuine support to others.

Individuals with higher KiQ permit themselves to rest without guilt, understanding that self-nurturance nourishes their best selves.

Listening Quotient (LQ): Engaging Through Active Listening

The Listening Quotient (LQ) goes beyond simply hearing others; it involves tuning into your own needs, feelings, and inner wisdom, as well as those of others.

Someone with a high LQ knows when to take a break instead of pushing through fatigue.

Non-Judgment Quotient (NJQ): Letting Go

Sustainable self-nurturance means embracing your true self rather than clinging to unrealistic expectations. A non-judgmental quotient helps eliminate self-imposed pressures, criticism and judgment.

A person with high NJQ views self-nurturance as a continuous journey rather than a fixed goal.

The Role of Affirmations in Sustainable Self-Nurturance

Affirmations are purposeful statements that significantly influence our feelings, emotions, and behaviors. Here's how affirmations promote long-term self-nurturance and how to integrate them into your daily routine:

Strengthen Self-Acceptance

Many individuals struggle with self-nurturance due to the belief that they are not worthy of love and affection.

Affirmations transform a negative self-image into self-acceptance, making self-nurturance feel more natural and valuable.

A Few Examples of Affirmations:

- *I love and accept myself the way I am*

- *I am deserving of nurture, rest, and love.*

- *I show myself the same kindness that I extend to others.*

Regularly repeating self-acceptance affirmations transforms self-nurturance into a guilt-free, routine practice.

Transform Negative Thought Patterns

If we repeatedly tell ourselves, "I don't have time for self-nurture" or "nurturing myself is selfish," our brains accept these statements as truths. Affirmations challenge and reshape these limiting beliefs, making it easier to practice sustainable self-nurturance.

A Few Examples of Affirmations:

- *Prioritizing my wellbeing enables me to contribute my best to the world.*

- *Self-nurturance is essential for my health and*

happiness.

- *I make time for what nourishes me and do so without guilt.*

Over time, these affirmations condition your brain to see self-nurturance as essential rather than optional.

Boost Emotional Resilience

Life's challenges often interfere with and disrupt self-nurturance routines. Affirmations enhance emotional wellbeing and resilience, allowing self-nurturing to continue even during challenging times.

A Few Examples of Affirmations:

- *I handle life's challenges with grace and patience.*

- *I am strong, resilient, and capable of overcoming difficult times.*

- *Even on challenging days, I choose one small act of self-nurturance for myself.*

These affirmations strengthen the practice of self-nurturance during stressful times, helping to avoid burnout and emotional fatigue.

Build Awareness

A significant aspect of self-nurturance is being fully present to the self. Affirmations encourage mindful living, facilitating the enjoyment and sustainability of self-nurturance practices.

A Few Examples of Affirmations:

- *I am here now, fully experiencing the peace and joy of this moment.*

- *I take a moment to acknowledge what my body and mind need at this time.*

- *I focus on what nurtures me in this moment.*

These affirmations ground you in the moment, promoting intentional self-nurturance instead of being hurried or neglected.

Promote Healthy Boundaries

Many individuals find self-nurturance challenging because they often overcommit, agree to requests too readily, or feel pressured to please others. Affirmations help reinforce the importance of setting boundaries and protecting your energy.

A Few Examples of Affirmations:

- *I respect my boundaries and say no when needed.*

- *I set healthy boundaries to protect my peace and energy.*

- *I choose relationships that nurture and inspire me.*

These affirmations motivate the mind to value personal wellbeing, allowing for the rejection of energy-draining activities.

Foster Self-Worth

Sustainable self-nurturance depends on a strong sense of

self-worth and inner validation. Affirmations reinforce the belief that you deserve nurturance and fulfilment, regardless of external approval.

A Few Examples of Affirmations:

- *I am enough just as I am.*

- *I offer myself the love and nurture I deserve.*

- *I lovingly allow myself to rest and recharge.*

These affirmations break the habit of seeking external validation, transforming self-nurturance into an inherent, self-directed practice.

Encourage a Growth Mindset

A growth mindset encourages individuals to welcome change, tackle challenges, and promote ongoing wellbeing. Affirmations provide a perspective where self-nurturance is seen as a lifelong process rather than a temporary fix.

A Few Examples of Affirmations:

- *I am evolving and growing every day.*

- *I am becoming more aligned with what nurtures me.*

- *I approach new self-nurturing practices with curiosity and an open mind.*

These affirmations turn self-nurturance into a continuous journey rather than an occasional task.

Mindfulness Practices for Sustainable Self-Nurturance

Mindfulness is the practice of being completely present—actively participating in the moment without judgment. When focused on self-nurturance, mindfulness transforms it into a lasting, integral part of one's lifestyle rather than a momentary task.

Here's how practicing mindfulness ensures sustainable self-nurturance:

Facilitates Emotional Reflection

Many people neglect self-nurturance because they are unaware of their emotional and physical needs. Practicing mindfulness helps us recognize early signs of stress, fatigue, and emotional exhaustion before burnout sets in.

By acknowledging your needs, you can nurture yourself proactively instead of waiting until you feel overwhelmed.

Prevents Burnout

Modern society often idealizes being busy, which can lead to guilt around taking breaks. In contrast, mindfulness encourages slowing down and embracing your need for rest without feeling guilty.

Rest shifts from being a reward to a necessity, helping you sustain energy and prevent burnout.

Deepens Gratitude

Many consider self-nurturance just another task on their to-do list. Mindfulness shifts this view, promoting a more enriching self-nurturing experience that enhances satisfaction and impact.

Self-nurturance evolves into a joyful experience instead of just a habit, encouraging ongoing practice.

Fosters Empathy

Many people give up on self-nurturance due to self-criticism or perfectionism, believing they haven't "earned" the right to rest or kindness towards themselves. Mindfulness can help transform this judgment into empathy, promoting sustained self-nurturance.

Pay attention when your inner critic surfaces and expresses thoughts like "I'm not doing enough" or "I don't deserve rest." Counter these thoughts with empathy: *"I am doing my best, and that is sufficient."*

Self-nurturance based on empathy evolves into a natural,

sustainable practice rather than something that must be earned or justified.

Strengthens Bond with Nature for Better Wellbeing

Spending time in nature is a powerful way to nurture oneself, yet many people rush through their time outdoors without fully experiencing its benefits. Practicing mindfulness helps you connect with the calming effects of nature.

Instead of serving as an occasional getaway, nature can become a regular, refreshing part of your daily routine.

Conscious Breathwork

Conscious breathing soothes the nervous system, alleviating stress and promoting relaxation. It serves as a simple but effective self-nurturing practice.

Awareness of breath becomes a natural coping mechanism, helping you manage emotions and maintain balance.

Joy in Everyday Moments

Many people pursue grand moments of happiness while neglecting the small joys that contribute to wellbeing. Mindfulness allows you to appreciate daily experiences, enriching your life and increasing fulfilment.

Instead of waiting for "big" self-nurturing moments, cultivate a continuous practice of discovering joy in daily life.

The Importance of Time Management in Sustainable Self-Nurturance

Time management is essential for prioritizing self-nurturance and mental wellbeing. One can focus on personal growth without guilt by effectively organizing one's time. Making self-nurturance an intentional part of daily life supports sustainable self-nurturance.

Supports Sustainability

A significant reason individuals find self-nurturance challenging is the notion that "there isn't enough time." However, effective time management can counter this excuse by purposefully setting aside time for self-nurturing activities.

When self-nurturance is integrated into your structured routine, it transitions from an optional to an essential habit.

Mitigates Stress and Overwhelm

Ineffective time management results in stress, hurried tasks, and fatigue, making self-nurturance seem unattainable. Effective time management allows for breathing room and helps manage stress.

Reducing stress and finding balance protect the energy vital for self-nurturance and wellbeing.

Encourage Discipline

A well-structured routine and daily discipline inherently include self-nurturance rather than adding it on at the end. Good time management encourages habits that emphasize health and wellbeing.

Following self-nurturing practices into everyday life makes them easier and more sustainable.

A Healthy Work-Life Balance

Overworking leads to exhaustion, which hampers self-nurturance. Effective time management brings balance, providing space for both professional and personal wellbeing.

Effectively managing your tasks allows you to have more time for relaxation, hobbies, and self-nurturance.

Facilitates Prioritization

Not every task holds equal importance. Poor time

management can lead to urgent tasks, overshadowing essential self-nurturing practices. By prioritizing effectively, you can focus on what truly enhances your wellbeing.

Prioritizing wellbeing transforms self-nurturance into a lifelong commitment.

Promotes Intentional Breaks and Relaxation

Taking deliberate breaks enhances productivity, reduces decision fatigue, and maintains energy levels throughout the day.

Short, conscious breaks help avoid fatigue and enhance overall wellbeing.

Supports Personal Growth

Effective time management opens up opportunities for personal growth and development, allowing self-nurturance to evolve beyond simple care to encompass learning, creativity, and self-improvement.

Nurturing oneself with a growth mindset ensures a fulfilling life and avoids stagnation.

Safeguards from Time-Draining Activities

Distractions, social obligations, and toxic interactions can take up valuable time. Effectively managing your time protects your energy from draining interactions, excessive screen time, and unnecessary commitments.

Protecting your time and energy creates space for self-nurturance, peace, and personal fulfilment.

The Role of Balance in Sustainable Self-Nurturance

Balance is essential for sustainable self-nurturance. It enables you to meet life's demands while prioritizing wellbeing. Self-nurturance becomes a supportive practice rather than a reactive fix by maintaining equilibrium in work, relationships, and personal growth.

Many people struggle with self-nurturance, often overworking or indulging sporadically, which can lead to feelings of guilt. True self-nurturance comes from balance, making self-nurturance a natural part of life.

Here's how achieving balance contributes to sustainability self-nurturance:

Supports Overall Wellbeing

Self-nurturance is an approach that involves physical, mental, emotional, and spiritual wellbeing. Neglecting one area impacts the others. To achieve sustainable self-nurturance, it is essential to nurture each aspect of wellbeing in harmony.

Balancing your physical, mental, and emotional needs leads to feeling stronger, healthier, and more energized for self-nurturance.

Helps in Energy Conservation

One significant reason people struggle to maintain self-nurturance is that they often invest excessive time and energy in supporting others, leading to the neglect of their own needs. Balance helps you realize that it's possible to nurture both others and yourself simultaneously.

Encourages Adaptability and Strength

When life becomes hectic or uncertain, many of us neglect self-nurturance. Finding balance allows you to adapt, adjusting your self-nurturance routines based on your situation rather than entirely abandoning them.

A balanced approach supports flexible self-nurturance, allowing you to sustain it during challenging times.

Creates a Fulfilling and Rewarding Life.

Sustainable self-nurturance involves more than just rest

and relaxation; it also includes personal growth, a sense of purpose, and contribution. Finding balance allows for self-nurturance, encouraging more significant actions.

When self-nurturance aligns with purpose and contribution, life becomes more fulfilling, turning it into a lifelong practice rather than a fleeting habit.

The Role of Independence in Sustainable Self-Nurturance

Independence and self-reliance are vital for sustainable self-nurturance. By nurturing yourself emotionally, mentally, physically, and financially, you create a wellbeing system less reliant on outside factors. This prepares you to tackle challenges with both internal and external resources. Sustainable self-nurturance fosters resilience and confidence while still allowing for assistance when needed. Thus, independence enhances lasting self-nurturance.

Builds Emotional Stability

Emotional independence means your wellbeing isn't entirely reliant on others' approval, validation, or presence. This allows you to avoid emotional ups and downs influenced by external factors.

Emotional self-reliance allows you to derive happiness and self-worth from within, enabling you to nurture yourself amidst life's fluctuations.

Impact of Financial Independence

Financial independence gives you the freedom to prioritize your wellbeing without constant stress. Achieving financial independence allows you to invest in self-nurturance, personal development, and enriching experiences.

Being financially independent takes away the stress of uncertainty, enabling you to concentrate on self-growth, relaxation, and wellbeing without financial guilt or worry.

Control Over Your Decisions

Relying too much on others for decision-making can cause you to become disconnected from your own needs and desires. By making independent choices, you ensure that your self-nurturing journey truly reflects your authentic self.

Taking control of your choices allows you to consistently prioritize self-nurturance and wellbeing without depending on others for permission.

Level up Self-Confidence and Esteem

Being self-reliant boosts self-esteem since you know you can tackle life's challenges independently. Confidence in your ability to nurture yourself inherently supports sustainable self-nurturance.

Having faith in your ability to nurture yourself increases your motivation to consistently prioritize your wellbeing.

Self Responsibility

A common belief is that happiness relies on external factors such as relationships, jobs, or life events. Genuine self-nurturance occurs when you understand that happiness is your responsibility and make a conscious effort to cultivate it.

By owning your happiness, you consistently prioritize self-nurturance regardless of what life presents to you.

CHAPTER 8

SPREAD THE GOODNESS: INSPIRE OTHERS TO EMBRACE SELF-NURTURANCE

Imagine illuminating your path with the light of self-nurturance, dispelling shadows of stress and doubt. Now, picture extending that light to others, guiding them to navigate their unique journeys toward wellbeing.

Inspiring others to adopt self-nurturance is like becoming a lighthouse, steadfast and reassuring, offering guidance, hope, and a safe space for those seeking their own inner calm and balance.

The Far-Reaching Impact of Self-Nurturing

When we embark on our journey of self-nurturance, something remarkable happens. It not only changes us but also extends outward, impacting the lives of those around us. Imagine dropping a pebble into a still pond. The ripples spread far beyond the initial splash, generating waves of connection and transformation. This is the essence of self-nurturance: when an individual truly cares for themselves, they inspire others to follow suit.

In this chapter, we celebrate the stories of those who embraced the practices of self-nurturance and became living examples of its transformative power. Through their journeys, we will see how small, intentional steps can spark profound change, not only for themselves but for everyone around them.

Stories of Transformation

(Names have been changed)

Raya's Journey: From Exhaustion to Empowerment

Raya was the glue that held her world together. Whether it was offering a listening ear to her friends, planning thoughtful surprises for her partner, or going the extra mile at work, Raya consistently gave to everyone around her. However, after a particularly grueling week filled with late nights and mounting stress, Raya realized she was running on empty. Her energy was depleted, her enthusiasm had faded, and she felt like a shadow of her former self. It was then that she understood she needed help.

Determined to reclaim her vitality, Raya sought the support of therapy. With guidance, she began to understand where she had stumbled and lost her way. She started her journey one step at a time.

In addition to following the therapy guidelines, she began waking up 15 minutes earlier to enjoy a quiet cup of tea before the day's chaos. Moreover, she downloaded a meditation app and practiced simple breathing techniques each evening to alleviate the day's stress.

Slowly but surely, she noticed a shift. Her days felt less overwhelming, her mind clearer, and her heart lighter.

With self-nurturance practices lighting her way, Raya's calm drew the attention of others. Her friends began to comment on this newfound calmness and asked her what had changed. Raya shared her practices openly, explaining how small, intentional actions had reignited her sense of balance and joy.

Her journey sparked curiosity and inspiration, encouraging those around her to explore their own paths to self-nurturance.

Rahil's Story: Rebuilding After Distress and Burnout

Rahil represented the perfect workaholic and overachiever. His unparalleled work ethic and boundless ambition were commendable, but they came at a significant cost.

Long nights, missed meals, and constant stress had left him exhausted and barely able to function. Upon finally reaching his breaking point, Rahil realized he needed a change.

A wise and caring family member pointed out that he definitely needed to take care of himself and his emotional wellbeing. Although Rahil was initially hesitant, his desperation for a solution led him to give it a try, which significantly transformed his outlook.

Inspired by what he learned, he took one small step: scheduling 30-minute walks during his lunch breaks. Those walks became his sacred time to disconnect, breathe, and reconnect with himself. The simple act of stepping away from his desk and into the fresh air brought him a sense of calm he hadn't felt in years. Encouraged by how much better he felt, Rahil began to explore other self-nurturance practices.

He started journaling to process his thoughts and emotions, gaining clarity through writing. He made gratitude a daily practice, which helped shift his mindset from stress to appreciation. Interested in mindfulness, he joined a local yoga class and discovered the joy of moving his body with intention. Slowly but surely, Rahil rekindled his passion and energy. The transformation was unmistakable, and his colleagues began to notice the change.

Motivated by Rahil's fresh perspective on balance and

positivity, several of his colleagues began to embrace their own self-nurturing practices. Rahil's experience sparked a ripple effect, promoting a workplace environment that prioritizes wellbeing and self-nurturance alongside productivity.

His story serves as a powerful reminder of how small, intentional changes can significantly impact both individual and collective resilience.

Sofia's Story: A Journey Toward Self-Acceptance

Sofia constantly battled self-doubt. She often felt that she fell short—whether in achievements, intelligence, or deserving love. With a relentless inner critic, she found herself trapped in a cycle of self-judgment.

Everything changed when a thoughtful friend discussed self-nurturing practices in detail and encouraged her to explore the concept. Curious and intrigued by her friend's persistence, Sofia delved deeper and realized she had been carrying the myth that self-nurturance was selfish when, in fact, it was a necessity.

Motivated by this insight, Sofia chose to adopt small yet impactful measures for self-nurturance.

Each morning, she practiced daily affirmations, standing before the mirror and stating, "I am worthy just as I am."

Initially, the statement felt strange, but over time, they began to resonate, easing the harshness of her inner critic. Additionally, she initiated a gratitude journal, noting three qualities she appreciated about herself each day.

These simple habits allowed her to focus on her strengths and develop a kinder, more compassionate view of herself.

As Sofia's confidence grew, her transformation became unmissable. Her newfound self-worth motivated her sister, who had also faced issues with self-doubt, to embark on this journey with her.

Together, they established a "self-nurturance circle" that welcomed friends to exchange self-nurturing practices and offer mutual support. This circle evolved into a safe haven for connection, growth, and encouragement, enhancing the impact of Sofia's journey.

Her story serves as a powerful reminder that even the smallest steps toward self-love can generate waves of positivity, uplifting not only ourselves but also those around us.

Key Practices That Sparked Transformation

These stories serve as powerful reminders that transformation starts with small, intentional actions. Here are some practices that made a difference for Raya, Rahil, and Sofia:

- **Morning Mindfulness:** Start your day with peaceful reflection or meditation to nurture a positive mindset.

- **Journaling**: Concentrate on the positive aspects of life to cultivate an abundance mindset.

- **Movement and Nature**: Engaging in activities like walking, yoga, or spending time in nature can refresh both your body and mind.

- **Setting Boundaries**: Declining excessive commitments and prioritizing personal time.

- **Supportive Circles**: Connecting with like-minded individuals for support and motivation along the journey.

How They Inspired Others

These stories are remarkable because the ripple effect unfolded so naturally. By sharing their experiences, these individuals inspired others. Here's how they achieved this:

- **Social Sharing**: Raya's simple Instagram post about her morning tea routine intrigued her friends.

- **Workplace Advocacy**: Rahil's renewed enthusiasm inspired him to advocate for wellness breaks in the workplace, encouraging his team to prioritize self-nurturance.

- **Community Circles**: Sofia's self-nurturing

circle became a welcoming environment where friends could share ideas and offer mutual support.

The takeaway?

You don't need to preach or push. Simply living your truth and sharing your practices can inspire others to begin their own journeys.

Call to Action: Embrace and Share

As you reflect on your self-nurturing journey, think about how you can share it with others. Here are some ways to spread the goodness:

- **Tell Your Story**: Share your experiences with friends and family or on social media. Your genuine sharing may inspire someone else to embark on their journey.

- **Host a Gathering**: Organize a "self-nurturance evening," where people can share their favorite self-nurturing practices or collectively enjoy a calming activity.

- **Be a Cheerleader**: Offer support and encouragement to individuals on their self-nurturance journey. Acknowledge their efforts, no matter how small.
- **Lead by Example**: The most powerful way to inspire is to embody the change you wish to see. Allow your actions to speak volumes.

The World Needs Your Light

Each one of us who embraces self-nurturance shines like a beacon of light, guiding others on their own paths to wellbeing and resilience. Just as Raya, Rahil, and Sofia have done, your journey has the potential to inspire change in ways you may not even imagine.

Let us create a world where self-nurturance is not just a personal practice but a collective value that uplifts entire communities. Your light holds the power to inspire others, forming a web of wellbeing that stretches far and wide. Together, we can spread the goodness of self-nurturance and build a future where happiness, resilience, and emotional wellbeing are accessible to all.

CHAPTER 9

GRATITUDE

As we conclude this chapter, let's pause to reflect with gratitude. If you are reading this, you have already embarked on the journey of nurturing yourself and discovering your inner light, which is no small achievement. You have chosen to honor your wellbeing and to extend that honor to others.

For this, I express my gratitude.

You are a lighthouse, and that is both a privilege and a duty. It signifies to the world: "I see you, I hear you, and I am here to help guide you toward safety." This role does not require perfection but rather your presence. By caring for yourself and embracing your path, you create a ripple effect of hope, compassion, and resilience.

I appreciate you for allowing this book to accompany you on your journey. Your light is powerful, and the world shines brighter because of it. As you move forward, remember that your dedication to nurturing yourself and your desire to inspire others make you an essential part of a more connected and luminous world.

Let us illuminate our paths together and witness the darkness fade into a stunning, shared glow.

www.ingramcontent.com/pod-product-compliance
Lightning Source LLC
Chambersburg PA
CBHW060536160726
47991CB00001B/346